W9-DIF-422

how to start a home-based

Blogging Business

Brett Snyder

gpp®

Guilford, Connecticut

Copyright © 2012 by Morris Book Publishing, LLC

Editorial Director: Cynthia Hughes Cullen
Editor: Tracee Williams
Project Editor: Lauren Brancato
Text Design: Sheryl P. Kober
Layout: Sue Murray

Library of Congress Cataloging-in-Publication Data is available on file.

ISBN 978-0-7627-7875-1

Printed in the United States of America

10 9 8 7 6 5 4 3 2 1

how to start a home-based

Blogging Business

Contents

Acknowledgments

Thanks are due to everyone who has helped me build my own business to the point where I can now write this book to help others do the same. Heather and Chris were instrumental in getting my blog off the ground. My wife, Kirsten, has been my sounding board and strong supporter throughout. Countless others have contributed in ways they probably don't even realize.

Introduction

So you want to start your own blogging business? You've come to the right place. It can be difficult to start any kind of business, but with a little help pointing you in the right direction, you can make it happen and be successful doing it. With the right idea and strong passion, the possibilities are there to create a thriving, sustainable business.

This book can help you narrow down your idea and turn it into something that can work as a blogging business, and not just as a casual and informal blog. Often, one of the biggest problems faced by budding bloggers today is the ability to transform an idea into something that can generate revenue. You'll find tips to make that happen here.

But before we get into that, you need to find out if you're actually fit to write a blog. Plenty of people think that they are, but they get frustrated when they get started in practice. With a little work up front, you can figure out whether or not this is a good fit for you, before you spend effort setting up the business itself. We have some quizzes that can help you determine how you'll do.

Once you have your mind set on creating that blogging business, the hard work begins. It's time to begin envisioning how you want your business to work. What kind of blog do you want to have? What will be your focus? How much time will you spend on it? Will it be just a blog or do you expect it to be more than that? Creating a high-level vision will help when you look to do things on a tactical level.

If that's all done you might think it's time to start blogging. Not so fast. There is still a great deal of prep work involved, and it starts with your workspace. Running a business is no easy task, and setting up your workspace in a way that makes you work smarter will be key.

When your workspace is set, you can start doing the real work. But that doesn't mean you'll be blogging right away. It means that you can start to create your blog. You may not have thought about things like the blog design, which blogging platform to use, and what kind of blogging you want to do (yes, there are different kinds), but these should all be addressed up front. That doesn't mean you can't change down the line (you should DEFINITELY adapt as needed), but it does mean you should start with a solid plan.

Then it's time to blog, right? Nope. I know, this is painful, but trust me. If you get it done right in the beginning, your life will be better in the end. This book will help you through all the tedious requirements for setting up the business itself. You would hope that it would be easy to do those kinds of things, but it's not. Setting up a business can be tough and honestly, pretty annoying. You need to think about how to structure the business. Is it a sole proprietorship? A corporation? Or is it something in between? You'll need to set up bank accounts and tax IDs. This is clearly the least fun part of the process, but it's a necessary step, especially if you want to get paid. (And if you don't, why are you reading this book?)

You need to think about the budget you have up front so that you can spend to set up your business. Depending upon the funds you have available, this will dictate how much you can spend to host your own site or have someone else host it. It will determine how much work you need to do yourself versus how much you can outsource to others.

Then, once you spend all that money, how are you going to get it back? It's not as simple as getting people to pay to read your content. If it was, I'd be swimming in a pool of money right now. But people these days often expect free content. That means you need to examine your audience to find out which model will work best for you. It's a somewhat daunting task since you don't want to make the wrong decision, but it's a necessary step. Some people will pay for content, and others will not. Which model is right for you? The answer is: It depends. (I told you this wasn't going to be simple, right?)

In here, we'll tackle some of the very difficult issues here surrounding ethics. While some bloggers might not think that ethics is important, it should be central to you in order to establish trust and credibility. It is very easy for someone to start a blog and make money by taking advantage of an audience, but it's not sustainable. We'll also talk about ways to balance the need to generate revenue along with the utmost importance of being true and transparent to your audience. That's a chapter to which you'll want to pay close attention. I think it's the most important one in the book.

Fortunately, this book doesn't stop with getting your business set up. We go into the early months to help with growth strategies. How can you grow your readership? What are some good strategies for encouraging comments? When should you look at using different tactics? A slow-growth trajectory might be easiest, but not everyone wants to operate that way. There are ways to increase your traffic very quickly, if you're willing to be creative. You can also do it by investing a ton of money. That might not be a cost-effective way to do it, but it certainly is effective.

This book isn't limited to your online efforts. You should think about ways to better embed yourself into the community you're writing about. Are there conferences you can (or should) attend? Are there events being held, formal or informal, that could help you to grow your ability to provide interesting content? There are plenty of opportunities out there, but it's a matter of identifying them and then taking advantage. This can mean late nights, early mornings, or everything in between. But it's something that you'll need to do if you want to really build a blog with solid, interesting content. Sleep is for the weak (and the lucky).

We'll also take a long look at the end of the book about your growth strategy. Do you want to keep it small and personal? Would you like to add other writers? Blogging businesses can go in many different directions.

Once you're done with this book, you'll have the tools you need to get your blogging business started and the tools you'll want to keep it going. Creating a successful blogging business isn't easy. It takes a lot of hard work, and it's not all fun and glamorous. Sure, once you establish yourself as an important presence, you'll get invited to some pretty fantastic events to cover. Nobody said there weren't perks to enjoy as part of the process. But even those exciting events become exhausting endeavors; you'll spend the hours afterward trying to put your thoughts into words while others can sleep blissfully. It's a very rewarding experience, and hopefully this book can help you find your niche.

This book isn't meant to be just a start-up reference. It should be used as a reference tool throughout the process. You will undoubtedly encounter issues along the way and need to look somewhere for guidance. The goal is to have this book be helpful beyond the very early stages of your startup. I hope you enjoy it and that the book enables you to create a very successful blogging business that you can be proud of.

You might think you want to start a blog, but you might want to think twice. No, that doesn't mean you shouldn't do it, but it means there are questions you should ask yourself before you dive right in. This chapter touches on the basics of what you need to consider before you decide that this is the absolute right thing for you. These are big questions, but you should be sure to get the answers before you start investing your time and money into the process.

The Big World of Blogging

Fifteen years ago, the word *blog* had yet to be invented. Today, thanks to the explosive growth of the Internet, blogging is one of the most common forms of expression in the world. In fact, there are hundreds of millions and possibly even a billion blogs around the globe. Anyone can start a blog and it doesn't cost a dime, but very few have actually turned blogs into legitimate businesses.

If you're looking to create a business around blogging, it's not an easy task but it's certainly possible. Over the last few years, blogging has gained more and more respect in the media world and today, many people rely on blogs for news and analysis. As blogs become more established (the Technorati "State of the Blogosphere 2010" noted that 81 percent of those in the survey had blogged for more than two years), their credibility grows as well. Nearly 20 percent of readers believe blogs are better written than traditional media. But the field is still developing, and that means there is opportunity for the right type of blog to succeed.

Competition is stiff. The blogosphere is a full variety of different kinds of blogs created for many different purposes. Often, blogs are meant to entertain. Famous sites like PerezHilton.com and TMZ.com fill those needs. Others are an effort to influence the political discourse. There are plenty of blogs on the left, the right, and everywhere in between covering every country on earth. Other blogs are meant to educate. These tend to be written by people who work in a field or have a specific passion for it. You'll also find personal blogs—journals that are meant to be public (or at least shared with a group of friends).

Of all the blogs out there, most of them actually aren't meant to make money. They may cover small niche markets, or they might just be done for the love of the game. While someone who decides to write a blog on the mating rituals of the naked mole rat might think he's going to get rich, he's probably not. Most people don't.

According to the Technorati report, nearly half of all bloggers surveyed had a graduate degree, yet only 11 percent made it a full-time job. Which means people do it either as a part of their traditional job or because they love it. The latter plays an important part in finding an audience. Readers follow blogs with strong, insightful content.

While content is a huge driver of success, frequency plays a big part as well. The top one hundred blogs on Technorati generate nearly five hundred times the volume of the average blog. To really make this a business requires tremendous devotion and a great deal of time.

Having passion about a topic is a great reason to start blogging, but there is a lot more to it than that. This book will help potential bloggers by asking the important questions needed to focus the blog. It will also set expectations so there are fewer surprises along the way. Making a blog a success can be a challenge, but it's not out of reach for those who are determined.

Why Do You Want to Blog?

If your motivation in starting a blogging business is to get rich, you might not be in the right profession. When it comes to blogging, content is incredibly important. To get that content, you need to have a passion for the subject on which you're writing or people will see right through it. Sure, you might be able to make a quick buck if you play your cards right, but to create a long-lasting business, you need to make sure you're doing something for which you have a passion.

Many people have passion for a variety of different things, but that doesn't mean that they should become bloggers or would even be good at it if they did. So why do you want to blog?

Remember that with millions of blogs, news sites, and networks out there, information can travel very quickly and easily. For most topics of broad interest, there are already plenty of news sites and aggregators that will get anyone all the information they need around an industry. If you're looking to start a blog that just reports the news, you might find it hard to attract followers.

On the other hand, if you have a strong opinion and can express it in a way that gets attention and participation from commenters, you'll have an easier (not easy) path to success. Many blogs have successfully started because they provide a unique angle from a passionate party. Of course, there's a lot more to it than just that, and it all starts with how you write.

Checking Your Writing Skills

When you think about writing skills, you may think about proper grammar and appropriate tone. Many people think about newspaper styles when they get started, but that's generally not what's going to bring you success in a blog.

Blogs are usually very personal. Even if there are multiple writers on a site, each writer has a unique style that stands out. Unlike in newspapers where the goal is formality and rigid styles, blogs are much less standardized.

For this reason those who grew up in a traditional newspaper environment will often not make good bloggers. Readers who want that style of reporting will usually go to a newspaper. People who read blogs usually come for the more casual, chatty style of writing. That can be a big change for professional writers.

That being said, it doesn't mean that a blogger should come in and treat writing like composing a text message. Proper grammar is still very important, even in a casual writing style. Sloppy grammar or poor spelling will turn people off immediately and make starting a blogging business incredibly difficult.

One thing you will find is that the written "voice" you put out when you start writing is not going to be the same voice that appears a year down the line. You have to start somewhere and you'll need to slowly adapt as you get the hang of the process.

Do You Like to Write?

It may seem like a funny question to ask, but do you even like to write? Nobody likes writing tenth-grade book reports, but that's not what we're talking about here. Did you keep a diary growing up? Do you write lengthy comments on Facebook? Are you

Writing Quiz

Here's a simple quiz to see if you have what it takes to get started:

1. I feel real good about the chances of the team winning the Super Bowl this year.

   ANSWER: Basic grammatical errors like "real good" make you seem uneducated and ill-informed, even if you're not. Do your best to avoid basic grammatical errors like these.

2. If the governor runs again I'll be really pissed off.

   ANSWER: Nothing. As mentioned, blogs are usually much more informal than traditional media. This use of language is likely to be found frequently in blogs.

3. When cooking chicken, you'll want to have a cutting board on which to cut.

   ANSWER: Though this is grammatically correct, it sounds somewhat stilted. As sad as this sounds, it can begin to sound arrogant when you use language properly. An incorrect usage such as "you'll want to have a cutting board to cut it on" may be better received, as much as it pains me to say that.

4. AFAIK, you're suggestion is wrong. Check the facts b4 you spout off.

   ANSWER: We have three problems here: While colloquialisms are fine, using too many acronyms like AFAIK (As Far As I Know) has the potential to turn away large chunks of your audience who don't know what you're saying. Also, make sure you use the correct version of different words like "you're." (In this case, it should be "your.") Using abbreviations like b4 might be acceptable in text message, but on blogs it just makes you seem simple and lacking intelligence.

Are you starting to get the hang of it? Casual but not stupid is the key. As I said above, you'll develop a greater understanding of your style over time. Never be afraid to ask friends and family for advice.

an active, participating member of discussion groups? Those are all great outlets for expression, and if you use them, you probably like to write.

But blogging is a different story completely. If you're going to blog, then you're going to have to write in tremendous volume. The more you post, the better chance you have of attracting attention. That can mean a lot of time cranking out posts. You may struggle for topics from time to time, but you'll always need to push through and find something to say. It can be draining and it's only survivable if you really like to write.

If you don't, even if you write well, you'll find yourself burnt out quickly and uninterested in continuing.

Will People Want to Read You?

We touched on this briefly above, but the most important thing you can ask yourself before getting started is whether or not people will want to read you. That's a hard question to answer, but you can look to others for help.

If you're planning on writing about a certain topic, reach out to people you know who would find interest in what you're planning. Explain what you're looking to do and maybe even pass along a couple of sample posts. Gauge whether or not there's even an interest in what you're doing and how you're doing it.

Your audience is, of course, going to be much larger than just the community you know personally, but there is no better place to start. Word of mouth is a powerful thing, and these are the people most likely to recommend you even if they don't like what you're doing.

Once you have a plan together and you've found enough interest, it's time to step back and once again think twice about whether or not you want to do this.

Understanding the Time Commitment

Blogging is not a nine-to-five job. It's a twenty-four-hour-a-day business that, depending upon what you're covering, can require long hours and tireless effort. So even if you have the right idea, good writing skills, and an interest, you should still think about whether or not it's worth it.

If you're covering a global industry and you're looking to break news, that can mean being prepared to write all day and night. Eventually, you can grow into having several contributors spread out over the world, but when you start you're going to want to keep much of the responsibility on yourself, if not all.

Going to Your Friends

Your friends can provide some of the best assistance when it comes to finding out whether or not people will want to read you. Here's a handy guide for how to go about tapping into that resource.

1. Identify friends who you trust to be honest. You really want to reach out to good friends who won't pull punches, because you need to know if you're not doing well.
2. Try to do it in person instead of over e-mail. E-mail can be misinterpreted easily and your friends can hide their initial first reaction if you're not there. You want to get first impressions and it's easiest to get that in person.
3. Prepare a few different types of posts that cover different areas of interest. Make sure you have an example of each type of post you're considering writing so you can get reaction.
4. Keep an eye on your friends and make sure they aren't in a hurry and aren't getting tired. You might not get the right kind of reaction if they have other things on their minds. (Feel free to pump them full of pizza and beer to keep them happy.)
5. Once you've received the reactions you need, rinse and repeat. I mean, make changes and go back to them again to see if you've improved upon your original.

That can mean some very long hours for you and not reliable ones at that. Are you prepared to fully commit to this? If so, then there's just one more question to ask.

Being Your Own Boss

How do you feel about working for yourself? You might think that it's the greatest thing in the world. No more bosses breathing down your neck. No more annoying deadlines or personality conflicts. You get to do what you want, so it's perfect, right?

Not so fast. Working for yourself can be agonizingly difficult. The hardest part, of course, is that you need to self-motivate. There are no deadlines except for those that you impose. You have to have tremendous self-discipline. When it's two o'clock in the afternoon or morning and you're tired, you have to be able to push through because you know that you need to get things done.

It's not just being your own boss, but it's also working from home. When you're at an office, you're generally in the working mode, and you aren't going to get easily distracted. (Okay, so you still have the Internet, but you get my point.) At home you have to be able to do work instead of sit on the couch and watch Maury Povich. I understand how important it is to know if that guy really is the father of that child, but if you give in to every distraction, you'll never get anything done. And without a boss regulating you, it's even tougher than you can imagine.

So make sure you have a great deal of self-discipline and that you're able to set aside a workspace for you to get things done. Even if you work at home, you need to find a way to separate your work life from your personal life.

If you feel comfortable with everything in this chapter, then it might be time to start your blogging business. The problem is: Where to start? Let's look at the big picture first.

02 Envisioning the Business

You now know that blogging is for you. (If it's not, then you've probably returned this book before you got to this chapter.) That means it's time to start crafting your blog's place in the world. This chapter focuses on the big picture, the broad questions that need to be answered. What is your strategy? Will it just be a blog? These are all big questions that require thought.

Where Do You Fit In?

To get started, you'll need to put together a plan for how you're going to make this work. The first question to ask is: Where do you fit in?

Unless you're writing on a very obscure subject, there is likely a great deal of online literature about your topic already. For at least a decade, people have been blogging about their passions, and the sheer volume of work that's already out there in public means you'll need to find a niche.

I'll use the airline industry as an example throughout this book since that's my wheelhouse. People love to talk (and complain) about the airlines, so there was no shortage of general discussion. There were several sites devoted to talk about frequent-flier miles and points programs. Other sites had been built as complaint sites—some as ombudsmen and others just to allow venting frustrations without trying to assist with the resolution. Still other sites were more generic in their offerings—more straight informational sites to help people with the process.

You'll want to look at this the same way for your industry. Take a look at the landscape that's out there today. Do a lot of research on what's being covered today and what isn't. Even more important, do research about what's being covered WELL, and what isn't.

Once you develop this view of the landscape, it's time to review and see if there's a good place for you and your ideas.

What Angle Will You Use?

After you've figured out your niche, the planning work is still far from being done. You then need to figure out how you're going to tackle it. What angle will you use?

For some, it may make sense to create a blog that's an information source. If you feel that there isn't enough good, wide-ranging information on your topic, this might be the right way to go. It's also helpful if you think you have access to more news than others—casting a wider net will help to build readership by becoming the place to go.

For others, the blog can be a mouthpiece—an opinion site that espouses the views of you and your contributors. If news is easily accessible in your area of expertise, providing a unique and thoughtful opinion on what's happening can quickly attract an audience. People are always looking for knowledge, and that can often be found in unique perspectives.

You might also want to think about whether you're interested in breaking news or in deeper analysis. For some, the idea is to get the scoop ahead of others and provide quick hits on what's happening. For others, it's more about digesting information when it happens and then providing a more in-depth review with a unique perspective. This can dramatically change the type of work involved in the blog—it certainly impacts the level of urgency around news gathering.

If you're having trouble defining yourself, then it's always helpful to put your mission on paper. Here is the mission that was put together for The Cranky Flier:

The Cranky Flier is a consumer-facing blog written from the perspective of someone who has worked in the industry. The goal of the blog is to provide an in-depth, opinion-based look at what's happening in the industry from the perspective of someone who has been both an airline employee and a traveler.

This mission is useful for several reasons: First, it helps guide you as you prepare to put together your content; second, it is an easy reminder to keep you on track if you're struggling with whether or not something fits; third, it's a great elevator speech.

For those not familiar with the concept, an elevator speech is how you describe your entity to someone if you're in an elevator with them. The idea is that you have no more than about thirty seconds to get your point across and get them interested. Having this kind of short blurb ready to go can only make it easier to explain what you do to interested parties.

This can come in handy as you try to acquire new readers, and as a way to interest potential investors, if you get to that point with your business. Of course, just having a blog itself is unlikely to get investors onboard. So it's important to think about if there's something bigger than this down the line.

Is It Just a Blog?

As mentioned above, a blog alone is not likely to bring the money pouring in for most people. One thing that has become very clear in the era of the web is that people simply do not want to pay for content when there's already so much free content out there.

There are some notable exceptions. If your focus is on writing content for investors, for example, there is certainly an interest in paying for content in order to get an edge. But if you do that, you make a trade-off. Charging for content will keep your subscriber base low. That's not a "volume" model but rather a "margin" model. You

Should You Charge for Content?

Every day, bloggers get fed up with not being paid when people read their work, so they think about charging for content. Does it make sense for you? Here's a quick look at the idea:

DO IT if your audience is willing to pay. Most audiences aren't unless there is real potential financial gain for those who have access to your information.

DON'T DO IT if you want a big audience. Very few people will actually pay for content, so you will certainly have far fewer readers.

DO IT initially or don't do it at all. It's much easier to stomach if you start this way. Even though you'll build a bigger audience by starting free, you'll make people angry if you aren't up front with your plans.

DON'T DO IT if you aren't technologically ready. It takes extra infrastructure to handle payments, so make sure you're ready to go.

IF YOU DO IT consider a "freemium" model where you give readers a taste for free, but you have additional content for a fee. It's hard to get people on board if you don't give them a taste.

make your money off a smaller number of people who pay.

Others look at advertising as a way to get revenue, and that does work in some cases, but it won't work for everyone. You need to have a tremendous readership size in order to make good money off advertising, or you need to at least have a very focused, desirable user group. The latter, however, does bring up some ethical issues, which we'll discuss later.

With that in mind it's important to think about where this might go. Do you see other ways to make money as a blogger? If you grow your user base, you'll then be able to have credibility. How can you turn that into a money-making opportunity?

This isn't necessarily something you need to know before you start, but it's important to have the right mindset. Think carefully about what you might want to do to grow your burgeoning empire. If it develops right, you'll have several different opportunities. You won't necessarily know what these are in advance, but you need to make sure that you stay open to them when they arise.

Decide if there are certain things that you do not want to do. Are you interested in writing for other publications? Would you want to set up related businesses? Would you get into merchandising? All of these become possibilities as you establish your place in the blogosphere, so you should at least be thinking about it.

One thing you'll learn quickly, however, is that things change and what might make sense in the beginning might not make sense a couple years down the line. So set a plan for yourself but also make sure that you aren't so rigid you're unwilling to change it as you go. Look for opportunities to grow the business and seize them when they arise.

To do that, however, you need to make sure you're committed. And part of that is knowing how much time and effort you're willing to devote to this new endeavor. What type of job do you see this as being for you?

Full Time versus Part Time

It may sound like a simple question, but it's not. Blogging is not something that you can usually categorize into a traditional full-time or part-time job. It's a hard thing to do, and it's going to take more hours than you expect it will. It will also generally require irregular hours, so you can't say that you'll do it between 2 p.m. and 3 p.m. every other day. You'll need a greater commitment with some flexibility.

That being said, you can put limits on your involvement as a blogger. Do you see this becoming a full-time job that you hope to support you? Or do you simply want it to be a part-time outlet that can bring additional spending money while providing a place to use your creative juices?

Most people say that they would love to blog full time, but it's not nearly as glamorous and easy as it may sound. Blogging requires a strong commitment to continuously put out quality content, even if it is a part-time operation in your mind. Doing it full time adds a whole extra layer of complexity because you need substantially more money to support yourself completely.

You can expect long, erratic hours, so make sure you're adequately covering the news of the day. If you're trying to break news, then things can happen at any time of the day or night, especially in a global business where it's always a business hour somewhere in the world.

The level of dedication required to keep a blog going is very high, and it's even higher if it's your primary source of income. Having a regular nine-to-five job may sound awful, but when you leave work, you're off the clock and can relax with family and friends. When you're blogging, you're never really off the clock. As with any small business, you might be needed whenever you're open for business. And with a blog, you're always open for business.

Setting a Timeframe

If you have all the basics worked out, then it's time to set a timeline for yourself. This means you need to decide how long it will take to get everything in order, but it also means setting timelines with specific goals along the way.

These are high-level goals, not minor ones. These are the goals to help make sure you're on track. At each point, you want to consider whether or not things are going as planned and whether or not it's worth continuing forward if they're not.

Here are some goal points you'll want to consider using:

- Finalize your blog focus/angle
- Settle on a blogging schedule
- Complete setup of your home office
- Complete business formation
- Choose your blogging platform
- Set up blog template
- Write your first post
- Settle on advertising strategy
- Finalize ethics policy
- Begin acquiring customers

These are all good points that in time you can use to make sure you're on track with your expectations. There aren't any external pressures, of course, because this is your own venture. But unless you set up internal goals, you'll have a great deal of trouble getting off the ground.

If you're blogging just because you like to blog, then none of this matters. But if you truly want to create a blogging business, it means constantly evaluating whether or not it's going to work for you. Keep reviewing your goals and eventually you will find that it helps to keep you on track, hopefully moving forward.

Now that we've covered many of the broader points, let's get into the details. You want to start a blogging business, but how do you go about doing it?

Set Schedule

Day	Sunday	Monday	Tuesday	Wednesday	Thursday	Friday	Saturday
Subject							
Posted							
Comment Reply							

*Posts scheduled to go live each morning at 3:45 a.m.

*Saturday post with links to places you've been mentioned outside the blog

Variable Schedule

Day	Sunday	Monday	Tuesday	Wednesday	Thursday	Friday	Saturday
Subject							
Posted							
Comment Reply							

*Post whenever news breaks or when you have a whim

*Saturday post with links to places you've been mentioned outside the blog

What You Need in Your Home Office

Now that we have the big picture items out of the way, it's time to start putting together a plan for actually getting your operation up and running. The beauty of blogging is that in theory it's incredibly easy to do and takes very little in the way of additional resources. That's why so many people find themselves blogging.

But when you're putting together a blogging business, you have to put more effort into the process than if you just want to start writing a blog for fun. How you set up any business is crucial, and much of that starts with having the right setting to do your work.

There is no set level of advice for something like this. Every person is different and so is every situation. Some people will be able to thrive in a chaotic setting while others need peace and quiet. It's something that only you can know for sure, and it might take some experimentation before you get to a point where you're happy with your setup. But we can at least look at addressing some of the key decision points along the way to help identify what you need to consider.

Your Weapon of Choice

When you're blogging, your computer (or your mobile phone) is your most important tool. Most of the work you do will be done through your computer, and certainly all the logistics of posting and commenting will be handled there. So how do you pick the right computer for you?

First of all, it doesn't matter if you choose a Mac or a PC. Everyone has a preference, but both platforms offer perfectly good tools for doing what needs to be done. If you've long been comfortable with PCs, then stick with what you know. If you prefer to worship at the temple of Steve Jobs, go with the Mac.

No matter what, make sure you're comfortable with the keyboard on your computer of choice. You're going to be spending a lot of time typing, and having a keyboard that works for you is important. You can usually get a different keyboard if you don't like the one your computer comes with, but you'll want to double-check to make sure that's an option before committing yourself.

You'll also want to consider what type of work you'll be doing. Do you plan on having a lot of multimedia work? In other words, will you be doing a lot with photos and videos? Is there a need to manipulate those things to prepare them for publication? Make sure you have enough computing power to handle some of these types of tasks. If you can afford it, pay for a fast processor and a lot of memory so you don't spend ages waiting around for that little hourglass to stop spinning every time you make a keystroke.

Portability

Beyond just looking at the type of computer you might want, make sure that you think about portability because it can have a huge impact on what you should be considering. Every day, mobile options become even better and more likely to be useful for running a business.

If you're on a tight budget, you might want to consider running your burgeoning empire off of a single device: your phone.

Is that even possible?

People have been known to run their entire blogging operation from their phones, and it can work. With the iPhone and Android devices now allowing for blogging apps to run on phones, it has become even easier. It's not for everyone and it's probably not ideal, but it certainly is an option for those who don't have a great deal of money in the bank to get started.

There are ultimately three different types of scenarios that could need different types of devices. Let's look at those now so you can start thinking about what will work for you best.

At Home or Office

Whether your home base is an office or at home (we'll talk about that in greater detail later), you'll need to have something you can use to run your business. Since this is your home base, this will not need to be a portable unit, but you might want that to make it easier for yourself.

The likelihood is you'll spend most of your time working at this space, so you will want to make sure to get a computer with a lot of power and a large screen. Go to an electronics store so you can try out some of the options that work best here.

Traveling

If you do a lot of traveling or you expect you might need to be on the road a lot in the future, you'll need to make sure you have a device you can bring with you on the road. While previously this used to mean you needed a laptop, there are now far more options out there.

A laptop is certainly still the most obvious choice because of its power and flexibility. If you get a good laptop, you can use that at your home base as well. Consider getting a docking station with a bigger screen and better keyboard for your home, then simply undock and run when it's time to hit the road.

But laptops have negative features as well. They're relatively big and bulky. If you fly a lot in coach, you will probably have trouble even opening the laptop fully on that small tray table in front of you. And they can weigh a fair bit as well. If you're going to be lugging around a laptop bag all day, it can get tiring quickly. You can even hurt yourself carrying that sort of weight for lengthy periods of time. Laptops also tend to only last for a few hours without needing a charge, and that can be severely limiting if you fly long-haul flights.

Some laptops are lighter than others, but the smaller they are, the less powerful they tend to be. You will often need to trade portability for power, and that's not a fun trade-off, especially if you had hoped to also use this as your home computer.

You may have heard about the option of getting a netbook for while you're on the road. A netbook is generally a very small laptop that weighs very little and has a small screen. In exchange for this lightweight design, you get a very basic computer with very little power. It can serve a great purpose—the lightweight, portable nature of the netbook makes it very easy to travel with, but it is quickly falling out of favor with most people. Why is that? One word: iPad.

When the Apple iPad first came out, it was a revolution for those looking for a visually stunning and portable solution to their problems. The iPad has proven to be a stellar tool, and it has ignited the "tablet" space as a viable replacement for a laptop in some cases.

The iPad and other non-Windows-based tablets, however, don't necessarily have the same flexibility as a traditional Windows-based computer (or a Mac). If you decide to go through with an iPad or an Android-based tablet, you need to make sure that you'll be able to do everything you need. This can include accounting software and any specific tools to your trade.

If you find that it works for you, then the iPad or another tablet could be the perfect fit when you're on the road, but there's still a third case to consider.

On the Fly

It's one thing to have a device that works while traveling, but what about one that you need at your fingertips at all times? A laptop is great if you have time to find a place to sit and spend some time booting up, but you might need to write a quick post in between meetings or while standing on the subway.

For some people, a tablet like the iPad might fit the bill, but for many, a mobile phone becomes the key to success in these situations. If you have a smartphone like the iPhone or an Android-based device, you'll be able to handle most functions you might need in a pinch.

Does this mean you will need to get three different devices? Absolutely not. For some, three devices might be perfect. For others, it's a mix and match of devices that will satisfy the need in all three of these situations.

For example, you can conceivably have a laptop for home and the road, along with a phone for when you need to do something on the fly. Similarly, another person might find that a desktop computer combined with an iPad will do everything that is needed.

The best advice in this area is to take several devices for a test drive. Go to your favorite electronics store or find a friend who has a device you like. Once you get a chance to try out different options, you'll have a better handle on what works and what doesn't.

Getting Connected

As a blogger, you'll quickly learn that being connected to the world is incredibly important. Getting good information in is the key to putting good information out. Because of that it's incredibly important to access your network as you go.

The basic level of that is having an Internet connection. When you're at your home base, that's easy. You simply need to set up a connection with one of several providers that offer high-speed access.

But when you're on the road, it's a different story. Sure, you can float from wireless hot spot to wireless hot spot and log on when you can, but that can add stress to an already busy schedule.

Some mobile phone devices can act like wireless hot spots and let you log on to the Internet from a laptop. It is worth considering when choosing your mobile phone. If not, you can always purchase a device that will let you access the Internet from just about anywhere.

There is no excuse for being out of touch in your home country, but when you're traveling internationally, that's a different story. Most mobile providers charge an arm and a leg for roaming data access in other countries. For that reason, you'll want to research other options before you travel across borders.

You can always buy a data card in another country to use while traveling, or depending upon your phone network, you can simply pop in a new SIM card so that your phone will work on a different network when traveling. The last thing you want to do is roam, so take all steps possible to avoid that from becoming necessary. Otherwise, you'll face big bills at the end of the month.

But connectivity is about more than just the physical connection. It's also about how you set up your business to stay connected to the rest of the world. There are several different tools that are useful in this respect.

The first and most obvious is e-mail. While you can sign up for a free e-mail address from places like Hotmail, Yahoo!, or Gmail, that doesn't look professional and is not recommended. (You can still use these services to handle your e-mail, if you'd prefer, but just don't use their generic addresses.)

Instead, you'll want to set up e-mail to operate on your domain. We'll talk more about that in the next chapter. Just keep in mind that you'll want a professional e-mail address like bsnyder@[yourdomain] or even just the less formal brett@[your-domain] will work. This will be one of the first things that people will see when you communicate via e-mail, and it will set the tone for the discussion.

But e-mail alone isn't going to be enough. You need to have your ear to the ground and that means participating in social networks. Here are some of the social media tools you'll want to consider with more to come about each in chapter 10:

Facebook

Facebook is the eight-hundred-pound gorilla of all social networks, and because of that, there is a great deal of information to be found. Make sure to sign up and "like" the pages of businesses or influencers that you think can be helpful. Participate in conversations and be open to new groups and ideas along the way.

Twitter

With each tweet no longer than 140 characters, Twitter might seem useless to get information on anything of substance, but that's a very short-sighted view of things. Twitter is actually a wealth of knowledge, as long as you follow the right people. Many people will tweet out links to interesting articles or information found online, and it can be a great source of information you might not find on your own.

In addition, Twitter can be excellent for identifying trends. Using tools like Tweet-Deck or Seesmic, you can set up searches to monitor using key phrases from within your industry. You'll see chatter rising and falling on a variety of topics, and that's fantastic for identifying what's hot and what's not. You'll be amazed at how useful Twitter can be for data collection.

LinkedIn

If you're not already on LinkedIn, you should be. LinkedIn is a social community for business networking, and the connections can provide tremendous assistance when you're looking for information. You can find people who might be friends of friends that could give you info you need for a story. These kinds of tools are invaluable for developing leads for data gathering.

At the same time, LinkedIn can be the ideal tool for generating interest in your blog. If you're already plugged in to the industry about which you plan to write, then

LinkedIn is a great way to spread the information to potentially interested parties that your blog is on the scene. Join discussion groups about your topic and start to build credibility within the group.

The previously mentioned tools are primarily broad-based tools. No matter the industry about which you're writing, these can all be useful in a variety of different situations. But within your industry, you'll need to look and see if there are other helpful tools that are specific to what you do.

In the airline industry, for example, it makes sense to participate in sites like FlyerTalk.com, MilePoint.com, or Airliners.net. These are very much airline industry-specific sites and these types of communities exist in one form or another in just about every topic area you can imagine. Do your research and make sure that you're plugged in.

A Comfortable Space

Getting set up with technology is really important, but perhaps we should take a step back for a minute. Where are you going to put all this technology? Will you have a traditional office or will something else take its place for you? The beauty of blogging is that you have a tremendous amount of flexibility in determining how you want to work.

The most important thing in choosing an office space is finding out what makes you the most productive. Some people are experts at getting things done in busy situations. Others need absolute silence. Which one are you?

Those who aren't easily distracted and can work anywhere have an advantage. If you are one of those people, you might want to start by considering the two lowest-cost options. If you have a full-time job and are planning on starting your blog as a part-time business, you might want to consider using your full-time office as a base of operations.

This first option will, of course, depend upon how receptive your company would be to allowing that to happen. But if you're really just looking to start off small, this can be a good way to go, as long as the firewall in the company's computers doesn't prevent you from accessing what you need.

If this is going to be a full-time endeavor or the use of your other office simply won't work, then you should consider the second option: your home. The biggest advantage of the home is that it's free to use, but it has the potential to push your sanity, depending upon the type of person you are.

QUIZ: What Kind of Worker Are You?

Everybody has a different way of working, and working from home means you have tremendous flexibility in how you set up your space. Here's a little quiz to help you understand what you need:

1. When you are working and you hear a sound, how do you react?
    a. Keep working as if nothing happened
    b. Stop momentarily then return to what you were doing
    c. Stop and investigate
2. When you're focusing on something, you prefer:
    a. To be in a crowded area with a lot happening around you
    b. To have the TV or radio on in the background
    c. Absolute silence
3. When you are doing work on your computer:
    a. Nothing can distract you
    b. Only someone purposefully distracting you will break your concentration
    c. Any movement will draw your eye
4. When working, you prefer:
    a. To be at a desk in a desk chair
    b. To work at a table in a more comfortable chair
    c. To prop up your computer on you as you sit on the couch
5. You are most productive when:
    a. You're in your pre-defined workspace
    b. You're anywhere in the house
    c. You're outside where you can think freely

As you probably surmised, if you answered a) on most of these, you prefer a more structured office environment. In that case, you will want to set up your office to have a desk and chair and be free from as many distractions as possible.

On the other end of the spectrum we have those who answered c) for most of these. These are fluid workers who can be comfortable in almost any situation. That makes it much easier to set up a home office, but portability is key. Make sure to have a laptop and wander as you see fit.

If you answered b) on most of these, you're somewhere in between. You'll probably want to have a structured home office, but you want the ability to move around and change your setting when the feeling strikes you.

Before you decide to stay at home, think about the environment. Do you have a spouse who is at home during work hours? Kids? Dogs? All of these can become distractions very quickly and are likely to prevent you from getting the work done that you need to do.

If you do have distractions at home, can you at least get away from them? In other words, do you have a room you can convert into a true office? If you do, you can close the door and get down to business. Even if you can't fully devote a room, maybe there's a study or living room area you can reserve for use during business hours. Any boundaries you can set will help create a productive space.

If none of these options work, you will probably want to consider an office outside the house. There are several different ways to approach this, and some require creativity.

With any start-up business, cost containment is important, so think about ways you can find an office space without having to pay incredibly expensive monthly rent.

Think about whether you have neighbors or friends who might have an empty guest house or garage that you could use as an office. Some people would be happy to earn a little extra cash renting out a space they aren't using. Garages can be converted into a working space quite easily, in many cases.

Alternatively, think about trying to rent an office in an already-leased office suite. Law offices can be good places to start—many will rent out a small office space for a relatively small price. There are also companies that specialize in acting as brokers to help rent office space in a variety of under-used office suites.

Get creative and try to identify places that will work for you. For some, that can mean looking for space within a few miles radius of your house to make it an easy commute. Others will instead look for space in commercial areas where they can be located near important contacts. Even others will want to be near an airport to make for easy travel when needed. Just make sure you have twenty-four-hour access to your office.

As long as you have a place to work, a computer, an Internet connection, and a phone, you have the basic building blocks to create your business. Now you just need to get into a rhythm.

Setting Up Your Daily Ritual

As has been mentioned, blogging is not something that will generally fit nicely into a set nine-to-five type of schedule. It requires odd hours and a willingness to jump on things when needed. That being said, it doesn't mean you can't start putting together a daily ritual.

It's always a good idea to introduce structure into your day because it can aid productivity. Even if you work from home, set a time when you'll plan on going into your office and when you'll call it quits for the day. The nature of the business means you won't always be able to keep the hours, but you should at least try. It will be important for your own sanity.

Set a time to start work and then create a list of things that need to get done. A sample morning routine might look like this.

8:00 a.m. – Arrive at work, check e-mail

8:05 a.m. – Identify urgent e-mails and respond accordingly

8:15 a.m. – Review news sites for materials

8:30 a.m. – Visit social networks to look for news

8:45 a.m. – Check discussion forums and communities

In that first hour alone, if you set a routine to go to the most useful sites, you'll have a clear picture of what's going on. That will help you plan out stories for the next day or so and review deadlines and workloads.

You'll never be able to structure your day perfectly because every day is different, but it's good to have a routine. A few other things should be squeezed into your day. The more regular you can be, the more likely you'll be to keep those things in your schedule.

■ **Exercise**—It may sound funny, but you'll absolutely want to make sure to schedule exercise in your day. Blogging is a very sedentary business, and you'll be amazed at how rarely you find you need to get up at all. If you're not careful, you can gain weight quickly, so schedule exercise and make sure you stick to it.

- **Administrative work**—It's easy to get caught up in breaking news, which means you can forget to actually deal with administrative work. Whether it's cashing checks, paying bills, or just reviewing your finances, these are things that need to be scheduled or you might never get around to dealing with them.
- **Long-term planning**—Again, it's easy to get caught up in breaking news, so you'll want to schedule some time to focus on the longer term plan for the blog. As you expand and have more people in the organization, you can devote your time to more long-range planning while others deal with day-to-day tactical work, but in the beginning you'll be doing it all. Don't get stuck in the weeds or you'll forget to keep steering the ship.

While you're at it, you might want to think about scheduling the end of your day. If you aren't careful, you'll find yourself working twenty-four hours a day and that's not going to work well if you're in a relationship (or want to be in one).

Try to set a stop time and stick to it. If you say you're going to stop working at 7 p.m., then you should do just that. This won't always be possible, but it will help you to prioritize. Figuring out what's urgent and what can wait until the next day is always something that's difficult to do, but it's critically important to your success.

If you aren't able to set boundaries and create routines, then you're bound to burn out much sooner than you would have otherwise. You want to jump in to the new job and give it all you have, but if you give too much too quickly, you'll run out of steam. Some level of moderation is important to ensure you're able to sustain a long-lasting business.

This chapter should have helped you get a handle on the basics of setting up your office and building a work plan for yourself. Now, it's time to really get into the details. Now that your office is all set up and ready to go, you need to chart the course to launch your business. The next chapter will help you focus on this next step.

04 Starting Your Blog

You have your office and the routine is set, so no more dawdling. It's time to start putting together the actual business. Let's start with the basics—things as simple as deciding what to name your blog are crucial decisions that form the basis of the company.

Naming Your Blog

A great deal of thought needs to go into picking the name for your blog. The name will not only set the tone for what people will expect, but it's also something that's very difficult to change. So consider your choice very carefully.

There are external considerations you must consider when naming your business as well. Most important, you need to make sure that the name you want isn't already in use. There are some easy ways to start this search, but first you need to get some ideas.

Earlier, we talked about the type of blog you want, and the name should reflect that. Let's say you have a site that wants to be taken seriously. You'll probably want to avoid calling it The Funny Clown or something goofy like that. (This is not valid, of course, if the focus of your site is on the clown and circus industry.) At the same time, a humor site might want to avoid names like Breaking News. Of course, these are just guidelines. You'll often find sites using nonsensical names that have wild success. Think of The Onion, or Amazon. If you only heard the name, then you would never know exactly what those sites do, but they've built strong products and the names grew to become identified with them.

Only you can decide if a name fits with what you want to be portraying to the public, but there are a couple of things to keep in mind.

Try to keep the name short. A long name is unwieldy and usually unnecessary. Find something that rolls off the tongue, so to speak. But most important, find a name that you can use commercially.

Research

If you find a name you like, the first place you should go to is the Internet. Is the domain name available? You'll want to make sure that as an online business, you have a good, easy domain for people to remember. So if you want to name your blog Drudge Report, well, you're out of luck. That already exists. (And unless your last name is Drudge, why would you even consider that anyway?)

You might be tempted to stick with a name even if the domain is taken because the business using it is completely unrelated. That's probably not a good idea either. Not only is the potential there for confusion, but it makes it harder to find your business. It can also have some unintended consequences.

Take the case of the Universal Tube and Rollform Equipment Corporation. The company's website is www.utube.com. Might not have been a big issue back in the day when the website was started in 1996, but then YouTube came about. Very quickly, utube.com found itself bombarded with people looking for YouTube.com. This ended up crashing the company's website from the crush of traffic, and it filed a lawsuit. Eventually, it gave up and moved to www.utubeonline.com instead.

If someone goes online to search for your business name, the more established business results are likely to come up as well. There are also the issues around potential overlap in the future. It's best to start with a clean slate.

Your Logo

You might not realize it, but your name includes a visual aspect as well. Your logo is really a part of your name and your brand, so it's very important. Your logo can say a lot about you. If you use a very elegant font with a lot of curls, you're giving off a fancy or feminine vibe. If you use block letters, it's a no-nonsense feel. Beyond the name itself, the other images that surround it have similar impacts. Is it easy to see what your business name is in the logo? Can people tell from the image what it is you write about? Your logo says a lot about your company, so be sure to vet that with people before settling on something.

Here is an example of my logo for inspiration.

If you aren't graphically inclined, there are plenty of places you can go to get help with logo design. I personally know people who have had success with 99designs.com. That company allows you to fill in requirements, which designers can then review and provide options for you. Not only can you get help there with a logo, but you can also send options out to friends and family to have them vote on which is best.

There are plenty of other sites that offer cheap or free logo design including www.logomaker.com, www.logoyes.com, and www.logosnap.com. Just be careful. The old saying that you get what you pay for is certainly true when it comes to logo creation. Your logo represents your company and you don't want it to look cheap.

That doesn't mean you are limited to using any of these sites. If you know any kind of graphic designer, then they can help. If not, there are always sites like Craigs list.com, which can open up access to a whole world of options. Try to find a relatively new designer and you might be able to get high-quality work for a lower price.

Once your name and logo are set, then what? It's time to start locking it in.

Registering Your Name

Before you settle on the name, make sure that it's truly a name with no real conflicts. The first stop is the United States Patent and Trademark Office. You can perform several cursory searches to see if anyone has already registered the trademark.

Caution: You'll likely need to hire an attorney for a comprehensive search. It's possible to do it on your own and file the forms, but an attorney can lend very helpful expertise.

Just because it's not registered with the federal government doesn't mean it's not in use. Check with your state to see if it's been created as a legal entity there. This will be important when you look to create your business legally. (We'll revisit this later.)

If you've found your name, it's time to start defining the site further.

Websites to Look up Registered Businesses by State

Alabama: http://www.sos.alabama.gov/vb/inquiry/inquiry.aspx?area=Business%20Entity

Alaska: http://commerce.alaska.gov/CBP/Main/

Arizona: http://starpas.azcc.gov/scripts/cgiip.exe/WService=wsbroker1/
    connect.p?app=names-report.p

Arkansas: http://www.sos.arkansas.gov/corps/search_all.php

California: http://kepler.sos.ca.gov/

Colorado: http://www.sos.state.co.us/biz/BusinessEntityCriteriaExt.do

Connecticut: http://www.concord-sots.ct.gov/CONCORD/index.jsp

Delaware: https://delecorp.delaware.gov/tin/GINameSearch.jsp

Florida: https://www.myfloridalicense.com/wl11.asp

Georgia: http://corp.sos.state.ga.us/corp/soskb/csearch.asp

Hawaii: http://hbe.ehawaii.gov/documents/search.html

Idaho: http://www.sos.idaho.gov/corp/corindex.htm

Illinois: http://www.ilsos.gov/corporatellc/

Indiana: http://www.in.gov/sos/business/2436.htm

Iowa: http://sos.iowa.gov/search/business/(S(o0dsud55cqdad2umdqikpdrq))/search.aspx

Kansas: http://www.kansas.gov/bess/

Kentucky: https://app.sos.ky.gov/ftsearch/

Louisiana: http://www.sos.la.gov/tabid/819/Default.aspx

Maine: https://icrs.informe.org/nei-sos-icrs/ICRS?MainPage=x

Maryland: http://sdatcert3.resiusa.org/UCC-Charter/CharterSearch_f.aspx

Massachusetts: http://www.sec.state.ma.us/cor/functionality/search.htm

Michigan: http://www.michigan.gov/statelicensesearch

Minnesota: http://mblsportal.sos.state.mn.us/

Mississippi: https://business.sos.state.ms.us/corp/soskb/csearch.asp

Missouri: http://www.sos.mo.gov/BusinessEntity/

Montana: https://app.mt.gov/bes/

Nebraska: http://www.nebraska.gov/sos/corp/corpsearch.cgi

Nevada: http://nvsos.gov/sosentitysearch/

New Hampshire: http://www.sos.nh.gov/corporate/soskb/csearch.asp

New Jersey: http://www.njportal.com/DOR/businessrecords/

New Mexico: http://web.prc.newmexico.gov/Corplookup/
    (S(dg5pqgf1f0i4qvegemajnhm5))/CorpSearch.aspx
New York: http://www.dos.ny.gov/corps/bus_entity_search.html
North Carolina: http://www.secretary.state.nc.us/corporations/csearch.aspx
North Dakota: http://www.nd.gov/sos/businessserv/registrations/business-search.html
Ohio: http://www2.sos.state.oh.us/pls/bsqry/f?p=100:1
Oklahoma: http://www.sos.ok.gov/business/corp/records.aspx
Oregon: http://egov.sos.state.or.us/br/pkg_web_name_srch_inq.login
Pennsylvania: http://www.corporations.state.pa.us/corp/soskb/csearch.asp
Rhode Island: http://ucc.state.ri.us/CorpSearch/CorpSearchInput.asp
South Carolina: http://www.scsos.com/search%20business%20filings
South Dakota: http://sdsos.gov/Business/Search.aspx
Tennessee: http://tnbear.tn.gov/ECommerce/FilingSearch.aspx
Texas: http://ourcpa.cpa.state.tx.us/coa/Index.html
Utah: https://secure.utah.gov/bes/action
Vermont: http://www.sec.state.vt.us/seek/keysrch.htm
Virginia: http://www.scc.virginia.gov/clk/bussrch.aspx
Washington: http://www.sos.wa.gov/corps/corps_search.aspx
West Virginia: http://apps.sos.wv.gov/business/corporations/
Wisconsin: http://www.wdfi.org/apps/CorpSearch/Search.aspx?
Wyoming: https://wyobiz.wy.gov/Business/FilingSearch.aspx

Choosing Your Blog Software

Fortunately, putting your site together is very easy thanks to several different types of blog software that are highly customizable. You just need to find the one you like best. There are two different basic categories of blog software: self-hosted or third party-hosted.

Third Party-Hosted

The third party-hosted blog options make it very easy for you. The two most popular are Blogger (owned by Google) and WordPress.com. On both, your blog is hosted for you. That means you don't need to set up web hosting, you don't need to install the service, and you don't need to keep the software updated. All you have to do is pick your design in the system and it's on autopilot. Sounds great, right?

While it is easy, there are some drawbacks. You trade flexibility for simplicity. With these options, you don't have nearly the ability to customize that you get with other systems. In fact, WordPress.com will provide you with a large number of designs from which to choose, but you can't use your own or really do much in the way of customization.

Newer systems like Tumblr.com allow for greater customization, but you always give up something when you don't host it yourself.

That's why these third party-hosted systems are not ideal. They work just fine for a personal blog, but for a real business, you need something that can provide much more in the way of customization. That leaves us with the self-hosted options as being ideal.

Self-Hosted

With self-hosted blogs, you'll need to pay for web hosting. When you're small, this is a nominal fee that can be under ten dollars a month. As you grow and have a need for more bandwidth, then the prices can rise. Ultimately, however, the price isn't nearly as important as the reliability.

There are countless numbers of web hosts out there, and it can be hard to know which one is good and which one is bad. Your best bet is to get a personal recommendation if you can. Talk to people you know who have their own websites and see if they have positive experiences. If not, go to the Internet and start doing research. The more positive experiences you can find with a host, the more comfortable you can feel about going with that company.

Just remember, there's nothing worse than having your website go down, so that's the most important thing to consider when you're evaluating hosts. Low downtime is very important. Redundancy is also important, so you don't lose all your information in a catastrophic crash. (You should back up your own data anyway just to be safe.)

Once you have your host, that might help you decide which type of blogging software to use. Most hosts offer "one-click" set up with a variety of different blogging software providers. This means that instead of going through the cumbersome process of downloading the software package and installing it on your host, you can just click a button and it will automatically install.

BLOG SOFTWARE

	Pros	Cons
Blogger.com	■ Owned by Google so good integration with Google account ■ Easy for beginners to get up and running ■ Free	■ Cannot self-host Blogger, must be with Google servers ■ Limited use of plug-ins available ■ 1GB image limit shared with Picasa
MovableType.org	■ Good support for multiple blogs ■ Strong customer support if problems	■ License fee ■ Smaller user base
Typepad.com	■ Easy for beginners to get up and running ■ Free	■ License fee ■ Cannot self-host
Tumblr.com	■ Easy to use ■ Free	■ For microblogging, so not meant for in-depth work
WordPress.com	■ Easy for beginners to get up and running ■ Free	■ Cannot self-host
WordPress.org	■ Free ■ Tremendous flexibility with design and functionality ■ Self-hosted	■ Slightly more difficult to get set up

One of the most popular blogging software providers is WordPress.org. WordPress.org is open-source software, which means it's free, built by volunteers, and open to the world to modify. Millions of people use WordPress and there's a great deal of development behind it.

Others to consider are Typepad.com, MoveableType.org, or newer options like Tumblr.com. Take a look at each option, read the reviews of it, and see what works best for you.

In general, these can all meet your needs, but it becomes an issue of personal preference. Some seem more intuitive to some people than others.

Once you've picked your software, it's time to start working on the design.

Your Blog Design

You've undoubtedly read plenty of blogs on your own, so you know there tends to be a standard style used for blogs. In general, you'll have the largest piece of real estate dedicated to the blog content, which usually is shown in date order starting with the most recent. Then, on either the left or right side, you'll see sidebars with related information ranging from links to other sites to advertising and more.

Just because that's the standard doesn't mean you have to set up your design that way, but it's worth considering. Since people are used to seeing blogs set up that way, it makes it easier to navigate for first-time users. That being said, you do want your site to stand out so if you have a better idea, then go for it.

Without question, however, you'll want to make sure that you are focusing on your content. It's important that people find the most important information quickly when they come to the site. But after that, there are many options of what you can do with the design.

Do you want a basic design or something a little fancier? Some sites like to incorporate Flash and newer technologies to add some style and moving imagery to the site. In general, these tend to look nice but they're far less functional. Keep that in mind when you're creating something that needs to function well.

How much of your content do you want to share? For some people the idea is to just have snippets of each post on a main page so that people will have to click in order to see the rest of the content. This is done for two reasons: One, it allows you to fit more article snippets on the main page to get people interested; two, it creates additional page views when someone clicks through to the article, which can translate into more advertising revenue opportunities.

What else should you include? Most blogs incorporate links to other recommended blogs. These are called blogrolls. Many sites use them as a method for getting links back to the blog as a way to help build it up. Search engines use sophisticated algorithms to determine how to rank results, and one part of that is the number of links coming in to your site from others.

For that reason, people will often link exchange—where you offer to link to someone else's blog in exchange for a link back from theirs. I don't recommend using this strategy. The blogroll should ultimately be made up of sites that you enjoy and think are worthy of a link. This is your content, and if you want readers to trust you, you should make sure that you're linking to sites you truly like.

Remember, your design needs to be easy to view, and it shouldn't be too "big." By that, I mean you don't want to require a significant amount of loading time to download a large number of images or anything like that. Fast-loading sites get people to stick around longer.

You also need to make sure your design is visible on all types of devices. If you use Flash in your design, keep in mind that many devices don't support the use of Flash (though that is changing over time). Also remember that many people may want to access your site on mobile devices. You'll need to ensure that your site is easy to read on those devices, or, more likely, you'll want to create a separate, simple design that is optimized for mobile devices. Most blogging tools offer a simple way to create a mobile-focused design.

Other things you'll want consider include an About page that introduces what you're about to the world. Also think about a News page that will let you highlight when and where you've been mentioned in the press. It helps to build credibility.

We'll talk more about an Ethics page and a Terms of Use page later on, but there's one other thing to consider. You may want to think about a search function. Once people get to your site, how will they get around? Sure, they can go chronologically through the posts you've put live, but more likely they'll be looking for something specific. There will usually be a built-in search tool but think about using Google instead. Google knows how to do searches well, and using the Google search box will make it easier for people to search in a format that everyone knows very well.

Microblogging and Podcasting

One thing that you'll need to consider a great deal when putting together your design is exactly how you plan on blogging. In general, the word *blogging* brings to mind a standard definition of a site that has posts. Each post will be date-stamped and will be primarily word-based but sometimes with pictures as well. The posts will be shown in date order with the most recent being displayed first. That's the standard definition.

But over time blogging has taken on more varied types of meanings. Have you heard of microblogging? Podcasting? They can all be incorporated into a blog and in

Here is an example of my blog design for inspiration:

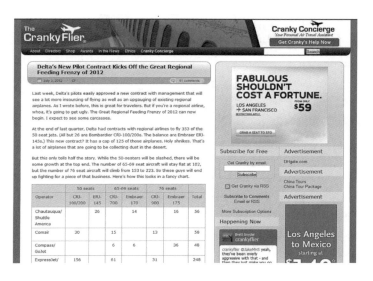

fact, have been successfully in many places. It's really a matter of deciding how much focus you want on each type of content.

Let's start with some definitions:

Microblogging is most synonymous with Twitter. The idea is that each "post" is very short and to the point. While a normal blog post might come in between three hundred and one thousand words for many people, you measure a microblog in the number of characters. As discussed earlier, Twitter allows no more than 140 characters per tweet, a word used interchangeably with the word *post* in this case. Most people won't come directly to a website to read a tweet, but it can be incorporated. Depending upon how much value you put on your microblogs, you may want to consider what sort of placement to give them on your site.

Some will just put links in the sidebar of the blog showing the most recent tweet. Others will work it into the main content area to give it more prominence. This should only be done if you plan on being very active in this space; otherwise it's irrelevant to your readers.

Get Your Podcast Up and Running

1. Record your podcast using any sound recorder, e.g., Audacity (http://audacity.sourceforge.net/).
2. Edit your podcast to include music, cut down for length, etc. (Audacity can do this too.)
3. Upload your podcast to a host and create an RSS feed using tools like Podcast Generator (http://podcastgen.sourceforge.net/).
4. Submit to various podcast directories, including iTunes.

What about **podcasting**? This involves putting aside the written word and instead going with spoken word. The name sounds funny, but it all makes sense once you learn the origin. When the Apple iPod became popular, people started putting together audio clips that anyone could listen to on their iPod. This exploded in popularity and eventually included video clips as the iPod grew to incorporate video into its capabilities. These clips became known as podcasts.

There is plenty of software out there that can be used for podcasting, but you really need very little to just put something out there. A digital recorder is all you need—you can even do it through your computer or your mobile phone (in some cases). You'll want to edit it down using some sort of software, and then you can put it live.

You might want to get more sophisticated tools depending upon the production value you're hoping to achieve. And if you want to do some serious editing, then you'll want to reconsider your computer choice—a Mac can make video editing much easier than a PC. And if you're hoping to do live podcasting instead of previously recorded, that adds a whole different level of complexity.

Podcasts can range in length from just a couple minutes to an hour. Some former radio stars like Adam Carolla and other comedians have found homes putting out longer-format podcasts that are effectively replacements for traditional radio.

This book isn't meant to focus on podcasting, but what you will need to consider is how much of that you plan on doing. You can incorporate it into the blog by just having a post with the video embedded, or you can look to have a separate section that will showcase your audio and video productions. Again, how much real estate you devote will depend almost solely on how much production you plan on publishing.

Implementing the Design

All of these considerations should be taken into account when putting your blog design together, but how should you then go about implementing it? There are several ways to do it, depending upon your level of comfort with design.

With many of the blog software providers, you have the option of using stock design templates instead of building your own. The beauty is, once you find a template that fits the basic mold of what you want to do, you can always change and customize it however you see fit. Many blogs have been successfully built from templates even though the end designs look nothing like the original templates other than their basic architectures.

If you have any basic knowledge of HTML and CSS, you'll be able to start making changes right away. But if you start getting into more complex changes or you'd rather start from scratch, it might be in your best interest to hire someone.

There are two phases to implementing a design. First, you need to have the design work done to show how you want it to look. Then you need to have someone take the look and turn it into actual code that will render properly on the Internet.

Some people specialize in one or the other, but other people can do both. Just find someone you're comfortable with and you'll be ready to go.

There are plenty of online marketplaces to help you find a designer and web developer, but just as with your logo, you can also just go to sites like Craigslist.com to find someone who is local. There's never a shortage of talented designers and developers who will be willing and able to help on a project like this.

You're heading in the right direction when it comes to setting up your website, but we need to step back for a minute. You need to make sure that you have the legal structure of the business set up properly so that you'll be ready to go when the money starts flowing in. We'll talk in greater detail about which type of business entity is best for you, but for now, let's focus on what needs to be done.

Setting Up Your Business Entity/Biz License

First, you'll need to create your business, or do you? There's nothing stopping you from starting your blog as an individual and collecting money directly. You don't need to register with the state, but you'll just pay taxes on earnings like you pay taxes on a salary you receive. It's just taxed like personal income.

Why not do this? The most important reason is liability. You're going to be writing and giving opinions about topics that could be controversial, and despite our First Amendment guaranteeing free speech, you can still cross lines and open yourself up to legal action.

If you open up a separate business, you'll be able to protect your personal assets from being seized in case legal action goes against you. This is incredibly important. (Please note that I am not an attorney, so I can only offer information based on my experiences. You should seek assistance from a licensed attorney who can provide you with the best advice.)

If you're planning on entering into ownership with another party, it's essential to set up some sort of separate partnership that will help divide ownership. This can also be accomplished in various legal structures.

State Considerations

Business creation is something that's left to the state, so you'll want to head to your state government to get set up. Every state has a website with plenty of information available on exactly what needs to happen to set up your company, but you might want to consider getting legal advice if you're looking to do something particularly complex with the structure.

What I found to be the easiest option is to set up a Limited Liability Company (LLC). These can have single owners or partners. I'll talk about the impact of taxation later on, but this is probably the simplest way to set up a company that affords legal protection. Check with your state for details, because every state will have different levels of regulation that explains what you can and can't do.

Which state should you use to set up your company? If it's just you, then it's likely best to set it up in your home state. Business revenues tend to be taxed depending upon where business is conducted. If you set up your company in another state, you'll need to pay taxes in that state as well as your home state since you'll be conducting business there.

If you have a partnership and live across state lines, you can look into what each state offers to see which one will provide the best structure for you. Once you get into more complicated situations and look at the possibility of setting up a corporation, there can be a variety of reasons to use other states. You see so many companies incorporate in Delaware. There are many reasons for this, some legal, some regulatory, and some tax related.

You can go crazy trying to figure out which option is best, so the best recommendation is to go with what's easiest. Once you're a big and successful company, you can always change your corporate structure, but when you're small, it's important to just get up and running.

Just because the state regulates businesses doesn't mean that's the only place you need to go. While you will set up your business with the state, there are things that need to be done on the federal and local levels as well.

Federal Considerations

On the federal level, it's all about taxes. If you just have a sole proprietorship and want everything taxed as your own income, you can use your social security number, but it's recommended to set up a Federal Tax Identification Number (or Employer Identification Number) that you can use for the business. This is completely free and can even be done online with the Internal Revenue Service (IRS) by linking to www.irs.gov/businesses/small/article/0,,id=102767,00.html.

The tax ID is still helpful even if you don't technically need it for your particular business. There's nothing bad about using the ID and you can still have revenues flow through to your personal tax return, but it just provides a separation between personal and business revenues. That will be important in the future so you should start with it early.

Local Considerations

On the local level, it's a different story. Most municipalities require a business license to operate a business within city limits. Sometimes business licenses can be required by counties or other local bodies. You will need to check with the local government in the location where you plan on operating your business.

Sometimes, a business license may not be required for a sole proprietorship, but if you are planning on creating a separate company then you will need one. Licensing fees tend to be for one year and can vary dramatically depending upon the municipality involved.

Many municipalities have complicated structures to determine how much your license fee will be based upon the type and size of the business that you're going to be building. Just follow the instructions from your municipality in order to make sure that you are in compliance.

Lastly, you'll need to think about whether you need to register a Fictitious Business Name, or a "Doing Business As" (DBA). In most states, you'll need to do this if you're operating under a business name that's different from the one you have registered.

For example, if you have a sole proprietorship, your legal name is the business name. But you'll want your business itself to be known as the name of the blog. To do this, you'll register a DBA. In some places, it's done with the state. Others do it with the county. Check with your state to see which is best. For more information, go to www.sba.gov/content/register-your-fictitious-or-doing-business-dba-name/ for a list of which states require what.

Your Address

We're making good progress on the business side of things, so let's look at some more details. What will you use as your business address?

If the plan is to have a physical office space, this is an easy one. Just use the address of your office if you'd like.

But if you're working from home, you might be tempted to use your home address since that's the easiest, but you might not like that. You'll be giving out your address for a variety of reasons. Companies might want to send you something via snail mail to review (if you do that kind of thing). Others will want to send you payment via a check in the mail.

The long and short of it is that you will have to give your address out to people and you don't really want that to be your home address, do you?

The simple solution is to get a post office box or some other type of private mailbox. These are available from the US Postal Service, of course, or at private entities like the UPS Store. The cost is minimal and there's bound to be a location near you. That means it will be easy to collect your mail and it will help you get out of the house every so often. That might not sound like much, but there will be times when you'll be searching for any good reason to walk away from your computer.

Bank Accounts

It might seem a little early to be talking about bank accounts since you probably won't have any money rolling in the door from day one, but it's never too early. If you're going to have a business, you need to have a bank account for when you do start earning revenues.

It doesn't matter whether you plan on forming a separate business entity or if you just have a sole proprietorship under your name. It's never a bad idea to have a separate bank account for your business transactions. This will keep it much cleaner for tax purposes, and that will become important when you start looking at deductions. You don't want to unnecessarily subject yourself to an audit, and it will just become more difficult if you do find yourself in that situation and don't keep your personal and business financials separate.

If you have a sole proprietorship, it can be as easy as opening a new account at the bank you already use for your personal banking. Depending upon the bank, you can even sometimes just open a new account right on the bank's website. The nice thing about this is you can then easily transfer money from your business account into your personal account. That's one of the nice advantages of having the same bank handle both personal and business.

Documentation for Bank Accounts

These are some of the documents you might need to open a bank account:

- Federal Tax ID

- Articles of organization

- Operating agreement (usually if multiple owners of LLC)

- Local business license

- Fictitious name statement

Each state may have different names for these documents. Just ask your bank directly to find out what's necessary in your state.

If you are setting up a separate entity, you'll need to open a separate account in the name of the business and not in your name. (You will just make sure that you're a signatory on the account so you can conduct all business with the bank on behalf of your company.)

Unfortunately, it's not as simple as walking in to the bank and politely asking for a new account to be opened. You will need to bring documentation about the company so they know you are authorized to set up the account. This can vary by state, but it will usually require you to bring the papers that show your company has been formed, among other documents.

You will also want to think about how you can use that account to accept payments online. For advertisers in particular, it can make your life much easier if you have a way to accept payments directly over the Internet. It will reduce the number of outstanding payments that are due by speeding up the collection process dramatically.

You can work with traditional banks on these types of things, but be warned that accepting payments online can be a very tricky and confusing process. It's incredibly hard to compare across providers because the different rates are so incredibly convoluted.

Accepting Online Payments the Easy Way

The easiest way to accept online payments is via PayPal or to a lesser extent Google Checkout. This is really quite simple. You go online and set up an account. This will act like a virtual bank account for you. If you're ready to accept payments, there are multiple ways to do it. You can send invoices directly to your clients and all they have to do is click to pay. Clients can pay with bank transfer, credit card, or with a PayPal balance that they might already have.

You can also set up a button on your site, which will make it even easier to pay. This doesn't make sense for things of varying value, like traditional advertising. It does, however, make a great deal of sense if you set up a directory or try to sell things of fixed value. The easier you can make it for people to pay, the better off you'll be.

Of course, PayPal will take a piece of every sale you make, but that's a trade-off you have to decide you're willing to make. You get a more stable payment system with faster payment collection.

PayPal may be the easiest, but it's not the only way to collect payments online. Nearly every bank can get you set up with a merchant account that will allow you to take payments, but then you'll also need a payment gateway that will connect with your merchant account. On top of that, you'll have to integrate the payment solution with your website. This becomes complex quickly and will require that you do work to integrate. Once that's done, however, maintenance should be minimal.

Alternate Payment Methods

Do your best to compare rates to see which works best for you. The problem is you might find that it's nearly impossible to compare rates, as there are typically three tiers of rates depending upon the type of credit card being used. It's hard to predict what type of card people will use for your services, so sometimes you might have trouble choosing between different rate plans. It's a very frustrating experience.

If you can avoid taking credit cards, you'll save a fair bit of money, but the options are more limited. Standard bank wire transfers can be very expensive with a flat fee. So they only make good sense if the transaction size is very large. There are, however, some services like Intuit Payment Network that have a very low fee for a transfer.

You can certainly accept checks as well, but that has several drawbacks. While there are no fees for accepting checks, you will find that it takes a very long time to actually get a check in the mail and then cash it. In addition, you won't necessarily know the people who are paying you, so you have to have a great deal of trust if you're going to wait for a payment to come in via the slow boat.

On a slightly different note, you'll want to think about having credit cards so you can make payments as well. Open a credit card in the name of the business so that you can keep your business expenses tracked separately that way as well. Business credit cards are effectively ubiquitous at almost any financial institution. Assuming you qualify, you can evaluate which credit card is best for you and just choose that way. This will give you a great deal of flexibility when it comes time to pay some of your vendors, and that's flexibility that you'll absolutely want to have. Besides, you can earn some frequent flier miles while you're at it.

Getting a Loan

One of the questions you might have right about now is: How are you going to fund this operation? Even if the expenses are relatively low, you'll still need to pay for some things, including yourself. If you haven't squirreled away a lot of cash to help you get through the early start-up period, then you might need to try for a loan.

The frustrating thing about getting a loan is that it's really easy if you already have a lot of money. But for those who need it most—those who don't have cash on hand—it can be difficult.

First, you can try your bank. Many banks offer lines of credit, which means you can use up to a certain amount of money when you need it. You don't get all the proceeds up front, but you can access the funds over time. Banks also offer credit cards, of course. That can be the easiest way to get funds, but you'll pay a hefty price in the end with very high interest rates.

For most small businesses, the US government's Small Business Administration (SBA) might be your best friend. The SBA guarantees loans, which means that if you qualify you can get access to loans you might not qualify for otherwise thanks to the backing of the federal government. For more on this program, go to sba.gov/category/navigation-structure/loans-grants.

Insurance

Not everyone in the blogging world carries insurance, but it's something that is certainly worth considering. There are plenty of examples of lawsuits against bloggers and the penalties can be quite high. You may want to think carefully about whether or not you need it.

Of course, you'll need basic insurance for things like your property and the like, but that's also what you'll need for your personal holdings as well. What you might also want to consider is some sort of liability policy to protect you if things go wrong.

There have been plenty of examples out there of a blogger being sued for libel. Libel is when you write something about a subject and that subject states you've written incorrect statements. Usually there is some sort of malice behind the offending item, at least that's the claim. To get clarification, speak with an attorney about this in detail.

Many bloggers will attempt to claim that the "shield" laws that protect journalists from facing legal battles while working also protect them, but that is not clearly true. It can vary by state, and there is a gray area on whether or not a blogger counts as a journalist. There is no simple test to determine status as a journalist in many cases, so this can end up being left to the court to decide.

Ultimately, however, even if the blogger is covered, there is nothing that stops an angry party from filing a lawsuit, even if it's completely frivolous. Attorney fees can start to add up quickly, so it's important to keep in mind the potential cost down the road.

For personal blogs, umbrella insurance policies will often help cover the defense in cases where another entity comes after the blogger, but that's not a guarantee. Every policy holder will need to check the policy for details. But personal policies will not cover business blogs, so it's not as relevant to us.

For your business, you can speak with your insurance company about liability policies to see if they have something that will cover you. You can also speak with companies that offer what they call "specialty" insurance. AXIS PRO, for example, offers policies for media. Whether or not this fits what you need is something that you'll need to review.

Remember, if you set up a Limited Liability Company, then that helps to limit your potential losses. That doesn't, however, change the fact that you need to find a way to pay for your defense and ultimately pay for a judgment if, unfortunately, it goes against you.

While this isn't a substitute for an insurance policy, there are some things you can do to help mitigate the chances of a lawsuit coming in the door. The most important, of course, is to focus on accuracy. Don't simply publish rumors or accusations that are unfounded. You want to make sure that if you're writing about something, you can back it up.

There's discussion about sources in chapter 9, but just make sure you document everything so that you can prove yourself in a court of law if needed. Also think about the subjects you're writing about. Some subjects may be known to be overly litigious. While you certainly want to make sure to cover every subject fairly and accurately, it will be hard not to take into account the nature of the subject when thinking about how strongly to word your writing.

Just remember, if you write the truth, then you have done nothing wrong. Unfortunately, that doesn't necessarily protect you from someone asserting that you lied, and that's why insurance can be a very good idea.

Setting a Writing Schedule

The basics are now in place. You have your focus nailed down, your design is all set and the building blocks of the business are in place. But there are a still a couple of things you need to consider before you get going. The first thing to consider is: How often will you be posting?

It sounds like an easy question to answer. "Oh, I'll just post once a day," you might say. But is it easy? There are plenty of strategies around what the right amount of posting is, and it's directly related to the type of content you have.

Blogs that are more about breaking news and less about analysis will often want to post more often. Short, quick bursts of posting will keep people coming back multiple times a day in order to make sure that they don't miss anything that's happening. If this is the type of blog you're setting up, then the more posts, the better.

Ultimately, you can become the place to go for breaking news on your subject if you cover it better than anyone else. That means making sure that you're covering everything that will be of interest.

When it comes to these types of blogs, you need to break the news as soon as you have it. There's no set posting schedule—just keep churning out posts with quality information whenever something important happens.

On the other hand, if you're focusing more on in-depth analysis, multiple posts per day might burn people out. Readers will come to your site in order to get educated on certain issues, but if you do deep-dive analyses on multiple issues then you're bound to be churning out a great deal of volume.

Some of your loyal followers will get inundated with the volume and that might send them away. In those cases, you might want to focus on quality versus quantity.

That means upping your quality by limiting your quantity. Try to do a great job on fewer posts than a good job on a larger number.

Having a commentary or analysis blog can also allow you to set a schedule instead of having to post whenever news breaks. For some people, posting at the same time every day can provide readers with a way to set their daily schedule to include reading your blog.

That might include set times once a day or twice day, and that can be good for you as well. It helps to introduce some regularity to the process, though you'll still always need to be ready to pounce on topics when they come up. In other words, don't force yourself to be too rigid knowing that you'll need to make changes when different circumstances arise.

With that, it's time to start putting pen to paper, virtually, of course.

Taking a Test Drive

Now you're ready to launch your blog and start building traffic. Or are you? To paraphrase the famous saying, "If a blog starts on the Internet and there's nobody to read it, does it make a sound?"

People start blogs on the web all day long, but that doesn't guarantee that people will actually start reading them. It takes some effort to grow your audience, and we'll talk about that in more detail in chapter 10, but let's start with the idea of getting ANY audience.

People will naturally stumble on your blog when Google starts indexing the site in its search results, but that doesn't mean you shouldn't be proactive on your own. At the beginning, it's a good idea to start floating your blog to people you know well who are interested in the topic.

Get some honest, strong feedback from people who are willing to give it to you. Sure, you can ask your spouse or your mom, but only bother if you think they'll give you real feedback that will help you to improve. Keep in mind that they likely don't care about the topic as much as you or others in the industry do (not always the case), so you'll want to get feedback from people who have that perspective as well.

Before you really start pushing the blog out there, it's good to get some posts under your belt and see how it works on a small scale. You will be better off having done this in a private group instead of making a big splash in the world.

The Internet is a fickle place, and if you don't resonate right away with someone, you might lose the chance to get the person as a regular reader very quickly. That's why taking a test drive is in your best interest.

Be Ready to Change

Even after you've poured your heart and soul into creating the best blog you can, you'll need to remember one thing: Change will happen and you shouldn't fight it.

Looking five years down the line, you'll probably be amazed at how different your posting style is than it was when you first started. That means you're doing things right. Keep responding to customer feedback and never be afraid to experiment with changes.

People like consistency, but they also like to see that you take feedback into account and act on it when it's the right thing to do. Maybe your posts are too long. Maybe there aren't enough images. Maybe there are too many images. There are a lot of minor things that you can tweak along the way, including the design.

Don't be afraid to adapt, especially since things online can change so quickly. There will also be that temptation to stay the same if things are working well, but that doesn't mean they'll continue to work well forever. Make sure you have a clear vision of how your blog is supposed to operate and then stay guided by that vision. (We talked about having a clear mission earlier.)

Now the blog is ready to go, but there is one important piece of the equation we'll need to consider: How are you going to make money? That's far harder than it sounds, unfortunately, but there are several different strategies that can be employed to turn this into a viable business. We'll look at those in greater detail in the next two chapters.

Spending Money

We've talked about how making money can be difficult, but there is one piece of good news. Costs for blogging are very low. In fact, beyond the nominal fees required to start up the business, there are very few hard costs that you need to pay along the way. As mentioned, there are plenty of free blogging platforms, so that's not an issue, and if you write content, you simply have to make enough money to make it worth your time. Here are some of the other fees that you will have to pay.

Hosting Fees

If you decided to go with a third party-hosted blog, there aren't any hosting fees, but since you're trying to start a business, you'll likely want to host it yourself. There are fees involved in that, but it's not that expensive.

There are countless potential hosts out there that can do it for less than ten dollars a month. You'll want to carefully consider each host that you review. For any host, the most important characteristics are reliability and speed. If you can't count on people reliably being able to access your site, you're going to have a lot of pain ahead of you.

People will not keep coming to the site if they can't get on to it. Similarly, if it takes too long for the page to load, then people won't stick around to wait for it very long. Some of that is in the design. Don't use large, bulky images that will take forever to load. But there is also the issue of the speed from your host.

How can you test these things? The best way is to get recommendations. Find people who are happy with their host and go with their recommendations. Nothing is better than a personal nod to a company from previous experience.

You can also go online and find countless reviews on web hosts. Just be careful that it's not some PR piece that was crafted by the company itself.

What kind of hosting package do you need? Well, there are a few different options. When you get started, you probably won't need anything too fancy. You can just get space on a shared server. Make sure you have enough space with the deal you get (that's rarely an issue), and run with it. You'll want to make sure there are frequent backups and redundancy to prevent losing your data. (You should still back it up on your own from time to time.)

Once you grow, you might want to start thinking about having a dedicated server. You can arrange this through third-party hosts, or if you really want to, you can set it up yourself. It's not worth considering this until way down the line, however, unless you're really concerned about having control over the experience. What you'll gain, however, will cost a lot more. This option is really not something you need to consider for a long time, especially if you aren't a tech professional yourself.

Paying for Content

Another real cost to consider as you get started is for the content. Will you begin by producing all content yourself or will you be looking to have others get involved early on? If you aren't providing it yourself, you'll need to pay for the content if you want quality.

For many people the motivation behind starting a blogging business is that they have a lot on their mind and want to start writing about it. So in the beginning for many bloggers, the content is self-produced, and that certainly keeps costs down. But in some cases, you might just have the idea but you want others to produce the content.

The most common way to do this is to pay per piece of work submitted. It's a freelance-style agreement where you pay only for what you need. Many different sites use this type of model to build up content quickly from reliable sources. The better content you want, the higher you'll pay.

Most of the time, these end up being pay-per-post models, though you can still find pay-per-word structures out there. For most, however, the idea of paying per post makes the most sense. You can have as much or as little control over this process as you'd like.

For some, the ideal setup is that you (or someone in the business) choose every topic and assign it to an individual writer to handle. Others ask writers to come up with story pitches. Once they're published, payment is due.

The cost can truly vary depending upon the type of writer you get. You might be able to find content for as little as twenty dollars a post but it's not likely to be of the highest caliber. Expect to pay triple digits for better quality, but you'll need to play it by ear. Each topic area might have a different going rate. It can also depend upon the type of content.

If you're just looking for a quick news blurb, then you'll have to pay less. Those are generally very easy to put together and don't require much investment at all on your part. But it's the longer, analysis-based posts that will begin to cost more. That makes sense; more time involved in creating the post should result in a higher cost to you.

Other Costs

If you're working from home and you already have a computer with high-speed Internet, then you really don't need to absorb any additional cost. (We'll talk more about what existing costs can be considered a business expense later in chapter 8 when we discuss taxes.)

You might want to buy a new computer, tablet, or phone as we discussed above. Those are optional, however, since if you have any computer with Internet access, it will work for you.

If you're leaving a full-time job to go out on your own, there will be additional costs in the form of health insurance, a benefit which would have been included in your previous job's compensation package. If you have a significant other, you may be able to get on his or her insurance plan, but otherwise, you'll have to go out on your own. Rates can vary dramatically depending upon your age, your health, and more.

If you are working outside the house, then of course you'll have additional costs that bubble to the surface. The first is, of course, rent. You won't need much space, so you can probably keep rent costs low, but it depends on the area and the type of space you acquire. You will also have bills for things like electricity, trash service, and cleaning services that will need to be paid. Don't forget the cost of outfitting the office as well. It can add up quickly, so you'll really want to make sure to do the analysis to see whether you need an office or not at this early point in your venture.

Start-up Cost Worksheet

Computer/tablet/smartphone   _____

Office setup (chair, desk, workspace, etc)   _____

Logo/website design   _____

Hosting fees*   _____

Business license*   _____

State company formation fees   _____

Business taxes*   _____

Liability insurance*   _____

Health insurance*   _____

*Expenses are recurring

07 Making Money

As noted at the beginning of this book, it is incredibly difficult to make a living writing a blog, but there are plenty of strategies out there. This isn't an impossible task, and there are proven ways to make revenue, but it requires really understanding the business you're in.

Some of the models might be contradictory to each other, and some will only make sense for certain types of blogs. So in order to really, truly understand what might work for you, it's important to really understand the type of blog that you have.

Charging Your Readers

The easiest way to make money on a blog is to do it the direct way—charge people to read your blog. It sounds so simple, yet it fails more often than not for one key reason: People just don't want to pay for content anymore. There are exceptions to that rule, but they are few and far between.

How many blogs do you personally pay to read? The answer is probably zero, or maybe one. These days, knowledge flows so freely that it's not hard to find free content.

Think about what the Internet has done to the media world. There used to be plenty of newsletters on a variety of topics that were sent via the mail. You had to pay for those newsletters, but if you were interested in a topic, that was the only good way to get information. Think about magazines. Sure, they made money on advertising, but they also had at least some subscription revenue. (That's still the case today.)

This model was much easier to sustain because there was no free alternative to getting ahold of this information, unless you count asking a friend or colleague to fill you in on the details of what you missed.

Throughout the 1990s, pay newsletters thought they had figured it all out. They could shift their publishing to e-mail and save a ton of costs, but they could still make money on subscribers. The World Wide Web had yet to develop into what it is today.

Once the World Wide Web came into widespread use, it changed the game. The costs of publishing and distributing information dropped to near nothing, and that meant that anyone could become a publisher. Internet access has only grown and every year, more and more people gain access.

You can now find multiple news sources providing news you trust for free online. The amount of free information is truly staggering, but not everyone is willing to concede that it should remain free.

Some large publishing groups have decided to charge for information. The *Wall Street Journal,* for example, charges $2.29 per week for the first year if you want online access to the journal. The problem with that? If you can't find what you want for free from the *Journal,* then you can easily go elsewhere to find the same basic information. Sometimes, you can even get the same exact information if syndication partners exist.

The *New York Times* is another entity that has struggled for years with how to charge for content, with several failed attempts. Its current plan allows anyone to read twenty free articles each month (unlimited browsing on the section pages) but to get access beyond that, it's $3.75 per week after an introductory period.

Does this work? It's not entirely clear, and that's why larger groups continue to try new revenue models in order to help pay for the larger, costly staff and infrastructure that was built during the time of printing presses.

But there is one thing that these entities have in common: They're both very large, well-known brands with content people generally find to be desirable. What do you offer as a brand new blogger on the scene? Not quite the same thing, that's for sure.

In fact, you'll have an incredibly hard time convincing anyone to pay for your content when you first start. That can, however, depend upon a couple of things.

If you've developed a strong following within an industry or topic area from a previous engagement, you already have a leg up. Some people have been able to parlay their fame and trustworthiness from previous engagements within the industry (or working in the media) to get people interested.

If you've been able to elevate yourself to that high level of standing in the industry, you can try to charge people and it might work. More likely than not, you're going to find that you can't make nearly enough.

Let's just do some simple math. If you want to make one hundred thousand dollars a year, then you'll need two thousand people who are willing to pay fifty dollars a year to read your wisdom. That might not sound like a lot, but it really is quite large. It's not easy to get that many people to pay for something that they don't know they need.

Another way to convince people to subscribe to your content is if subscribing will help them make more money. That's why you can still see a lot of success in the financial world. There are still plenty of pay newsletters that focus on stocks and finance. People subscribe because they think they can make more money by getting hot stock tips.

Another reason people will pay to subscribe is if it will help their career. Blogs that are internally focused within an industry might get people willing to pay if most readers work within the industry (as opposed to being customers of the industry) and are looking to get a leg up.

With either of these types of blogs, you might be able to charge your readers, but you certainly will lose a great deal of your potential audience. The question is whether or not you'll be able to earn enough off the smaller numbers to make it viable. If not, then you'll want to consider alternatives.

The Freemium Model

One model that has been used in many cases, including the *New York Times* as mentioned previously, is the freemium model. The idea is that some base level of access will be free so you will continue to have people coming in the front door, but there is a premium that's charged for full access to all content on the site.

This can work in one of several ways, and only you'll be able to decide if it's the right model for you. For some, there is segregated content. That means that certain articles are free to read while others require a subscription. The idea here is to get enough interest from your free content that people will want to pay for more.

The hardest part about this model is determining what constitutes free content versus paid content. Where do you draw the line and what's the differentiator? Sometimes it's the basic news stories that are free but the analysis pieces cost money. Other times, it's just a certain number of articles that are free each month and to get more, you have to pay.

In other instances, people will charge for full access to archived posts. It might be free for the first two weeks, then it costs for anything older than that. Sometimes it's not the content at all.

You'll see some freemium models where paying a subscription allows you to read all the posts without any ads in the way. Sometimes it gets you premium access. For example, maybe paid subscribers get quicker response times if they have questions. Or maybe you give the paid subscribers access to consultations that wouldn't be available to others. You could also look to offer discounts or some other sort of ancillary service for those who pay.

For this model to work, the free content still has to be compelling enough to draw people into the site, but the additional paid amount must be even more compelling so as to get people to pay. It's a very difficult model to make work, but you can play around with the different offerings you're hoping to make available to determine whether or not this is something that would work for you and your site.

Donations

For some blogs, you might want to consider a donation model. This can be very difficult to make work, but if it does, then it's a great thing.

Instead of charging readers, you can try to use this method, which has you request donations from readers to help keep the site going. Think of it as the National Public Radio (NPR) model of funding.

The method of requesting donations can vary. Some people will just put a little link on the side of the blog. Others sites have even used pledge drives to try to help generate funds. It's a model that is usually unsuccessful, and many readers are turned off by these types of open pleas. It has the potential to hurt the trust you're

Taking Donations

Way back in 2005, Jason Kottke did an experiment on Kottke.org. He did a pledge drive and was able to raise enough money in one month to replace about one-third of his previous salary. Jason had a large following but he was surprised that he only saw one in three hundred readers donate to the cause. And while he was able to raise a fair amount of money (though I don't know what his previous salary was), he was highly skeptical that this would continue to work year after year. You can read more about his reflections at http://kottke.org/05/04/micropatron-report.

trying to build with your readership. If there's too much pressure and people think they have to donate in order to read, they'll just walk away.

The biggest hurdle to making this model a success is the fact that blogs are rarely nonprofit organizations. When people tend to think of donating, they usually think about donating to charities, or nonprofits. It makes them feel good and it's a tax write-off.

This isn't to say that you can't become a nonprofit, but a great deal of work is involved. If you decide that you would like to angle your blog to be more of an advocacy group that works on behalf of certain people, then you might want to look into becoming a nonprofit. Even just writing about a subject and providing information to the public can be considered enough to be a nonprofit as well.

This book isn't meant to give you details on becoming a nonprofit, but there are plenty of guides that can help you through the process. Just keep in mind that becoming a nonprofit takes a great deal of work and requires a much higher level of oversight, especially since tax breaks are involved. That doesn't mean this isn't the right way to go for you, but you'll want to be prepared for the extra burden.

For everyone else, the donation button is not likely to be successful, especially not for a start-up trying to establish credibility in the world. There's a very small chance that it can work if, down the line, you've built up a large following and you don't have advertising or any other form of revenue generation on your site. But that's not something you should concern yourself with as you get started.

Advertising

The most common way to make money on your blog is via advertising. This is one of the most common methods for revenue generation throughout the world of media, and blogging is no different. Before you jump in and start selling ads for Viagra and the like, there are a lot of things to be considered when thinking about advertising. Let's start with the basics.

There are varieties of analytics you can use, and we'll get into details later on. But first, let's talk about what matters in advertising.

Advertising Basics

The most basic type of advertising is for you to sell a spot for a certain amount of time. Pricing on this will largely be determined by how desirable your site is to the potential advertiser. And that is usually based upon the amount of traffic you get, especially in desirable categories.

For that reason, advertising is often based on a certain cost over a certain metric. The lowest unit price in advertising is usually the cost-per-thousand impressions (CPM) metric. Every time an ad is displayed, it counts as one impression. Some advertisers will be willing to pay a certain amount of money for just the basic impression.

The amount you can make for this kind of advertising is fairly minor unless you start generating a larger number of page views. CPMs can run from under one dollar to double digits depending upon how targeted your content is.

If you have a very narrow focus, then you become desirable for advertisers who want to reach that particular group. If you have a broader focus, then you won't be able to get as much for the impressions.

The next level up is one of the most common pricing models, the cost per click (CPC). In this scenario, impressions mean nothing. You could display the ad ten million times, but you only get paid if someone clicks on the ad to interact with it. Why is that popular? CPC models show at least some interest in the product whereas CPM models guarantee no such thing.

With CPM you might show the ad one hundred times and nobody will even see it. But with the CPC model, you guarantee that there was at least enough interest from the reader to click to find out more. Of course, there will be fewer clicks than impressions, but in exchange, you'll be able to charge more per click.

This model is so popular because it is the chosen weapon of Google AdWords. You've undoubtedly seen Google AdWords on nearly every website you visit. The traditional Google ad is a text-based module that has a linked title and a short description down below. Google has moved on to offer other types of ads as well, including images, but the enduring text ads continue to be everywhere on the Internet.

Ad Sources

If you're interested in putting advertising on the blog, then Google is a great place to start. There is no minimum number of page views, and you can get used to working with advertising on the blog. You don't have to worry about finding inventory yourself but you can just let Google use its algorithms to determine the best ads to place on your site from the existing inventory you have. It's very easy.

For CPC ads, you can get one dollar or more per click, again depending upon how desirable your inventory ends up being to advertisers. There have been stories in the past of firms paying hundreds of dollars just for one click on very desirable, targeted keywords that have the potential to pay tons of money if a reader becomes a customer, but that is uncommon.

Affiliate Programs Can Help

Here are a few affiliate program managers you might want to consider when designing your ad spaces. Think about which offerings would help generate sales for the company, which in turn means money for you.

- AffiliateManager: www.affiliatemanager.com
- Commission Junction: www.cj.com
- FlexOffers: www.flexoffers.com
- LinkShare: www.linkshare.com

Keep in mind that many companies, especially larger ones, may manage their own affiliate programs. If you have a specific company or product in mind, go directly to the source to sign yourself up and start earning. You'll quickly find that some affiliate programs aren't worthwhile because of the low payouts, but there are some notable exceptions. If you have a business that can promote credit cards, for example, those can pay a significant amount of money for each customer that you refer.

Beyond CPC, there is another metric-based advertising scheme and it's called cost per acquisition (CPA). In this model, even if someone clicks on the ad, you still won't get paid. The only way to get paid is if the reader completes a task, which can be different for every company. In general, the CPA pays when the reader completes a transaction with the advertising company. Advertisers love this model because they only pay when they acquire a new customer.

There's no risk for advertisers to do this, and that's why it's easy to get these kinds of deals. In fact, you'll see plenty of "affiliate" program managers where you can go and see a list of all kinds of CPA offers. You can pick and choose which ones you want to offer and they provide the creative elements for you to basically cut and paste into your blog.

One other thing about CPA is prices won't vary depending upon how desirable your blog is when you're small. As long as you convert readers into customers for the company, you'll get paid a flat amount. That puts the onus on you to determine how hard to push the affiliate partners in order to start generating revenue. (There are some limited exceptions here if you grow quickly—top producers for affiliates can often negotiate better rates.)

As you start to develop more and more credibility in your industry, you will get more and more offers from people who want to pay on CPA terms. The reason? They want the free advertising on your blog, knowing that they only have to pay when someone signs up for their service. They have nothing to lose, but just getting something on your site will be a victory for them. For that reason, you'll want to be careful.

In fact, you'll want to be incredibly careful with how you set up advertising on your site. It's easy to start accepting every advertisement that comes your way with the hope that you'll be able to build up revenues through quantity instead of quality. That's going to be very tempting, especially when you first start getting interest, but it's best to have a plan.

Designing Ad Spaces

Create an outline using your site design to determine exactly what you want to offer as advertising and what you want to keep separate. Though you can charge more for ads that aren't clearly marked as ads, is that something you really want to allow on your site? For credibility purposes, you'll want to make sure ads are clearly marked as such and you'll want to try to avoid mixing ads and content unless it is incredibly clear which is which.

If there's confusion around what is an ad and what is your editorial content, you're going to lose credibility, or fail to even establish it in the first place.

You will also want to consider what types of ads to display. Do you want to allow only display ads with images? Would you rather have only text ads? Will you allow video? How about site overlays that blanket the content with an ad? (Clicking will make it go away.) As a general rule of thumb, the more intrusive and obnoxious the ad, the higher you can charge to place it. The tradeoff, however, is that you run the risk of alienating your readers if you put too much on your site in too intrusive a manner.

Your best bet is to find websites that you trust and admire, then pattern your use of ads after what those sites have done. Similarly, you should take a look at websites you don't like or don't find trustworthy. Examine the type of advertising they have and you'll probably start to see a pattern. If you stick with your instincts about these things, you're likely to come up with a functional design that creates trust with your readers.

Just make sure to keep monitoring your traffic as you go. If you see visitor numbers fall off or fail to grow, then you might need to consider a change. Analytics is very important to keep an eye on for the overall health of the blog. Let's talk more about that.

Analytics

There are many programs that can look at the performance of your site, and it's important to use at least one of them. Some are completely free, like Google Analytics, and only require that you put the code into your site. Once there, the software can track everything you need.

What will you find? Analytics software can give you all sorts of details, including some you'll be surprised to find are possible to suss out.

You can find basic data on your visitors including the number of page views, the number of visits, and the number of visitors.

Page views show every time that a page is loaded. One visit is the total number of page views that were viewed in one session on one computer. One visitor may have several visits over the course of the time period that you use.

Each have different uses in the advertising world. Page views show the general size of your site and more accurately reflect impressions. Meanwhile, visits show how many different times people are engaged during the time period. Visitors are helpful in knowing the total potential audience size.

But these metrics just scratch the surface. There is also a way to get more information about your visitors. How many of them are new? How long do they stay when they come to the site? How many pages do they visit? These are all statistics that help determine the desirability of your site.

You can look at what languages people speak to determine who you should be catering to with your efforts. You can also look at geographic location of your visitors so that at least you can see where their computers say they are. You can even see what type of browsers people use, what their screen resolution looks like, and whether or not they have browsers with Flash support.

All of these things should be studied so you can make sure that your ads will work when your readers come to the site. The goal for any site is to get high conversions for advertisers. That will get advertisers to come back again and again and pay more to advertise every time. So if you accept an ad that looks great on certain screen resolutions but not others, you're going to alienate your potential audience, or at least a big chunk of it. That's why studying your site performance is important.

You will also want to keep an eye on mobile usage. As mobile becomes more and more important, you'll need to pay closer attention to what goes on your site. Mobile advertising can be a different world with different rules and you need to know if you have a larger number of mobile visitors. If not, then it's not an issue. If so, you'll need to spend more time on optimizing the site for mobile visitors.

Analytics can also tell you more beyond your visitors' performance on your site and look at their performance beyond your site.

Where are your readers coming from? Where are they going when they leave? Those are basic questions, but they tell you a great deal.

If a large number of people are coming directly to your site, that's a good sign that you have built a large amount of credibility. On the other hand, you also want to generate a lot of traffic that gets referred from other sites. That means you have enough interest and enough linking from other sites to build traffic from various places around the web.

A third great source of traffic is from search engines. An entire book can be (and has been) written about search engine optimization (SEO) and how to make your site more attractive to search engines like Google. The higher you rank in search engines, the more people will come to your site without you having to pay for traffic. We'll talk about this more in chapter 10.

This kind of data can be overwhelming to review, but it can be used in bite-sized chunks. Let's say you write a single post. You can go in and look at how it performed. Then you can look at how the next post performed in relation to that first post. You can soon see patterns develop and you'll be able to make adjustments to your site to help drive more quality traffic.

In reality, small, actionable data can be more helpful for figuring out what to change on your site than the big picture data. But it's that big picture data that will be more interesting to advertisers.

Directory

This type of advertising is a little different and so it deserves its own section. You can set up a paid directory that will help companies to list themselves as a way to reach your readers.

The directory option can be one of the most popular types of advertising because it's a cheap way to reach readers on your site. It won't generate a tremendous amount of revenue from each sale, but it can create a steady source of income. If you have a lot of directory advertisers, it can become quite lucrative.

When setting up a directory, you'll want to link it to a prominent spot on the home page. You want to make sure that your readers know you have a directory and that they go to visit it when they need something.

Here is an example of a directory from my own blog:

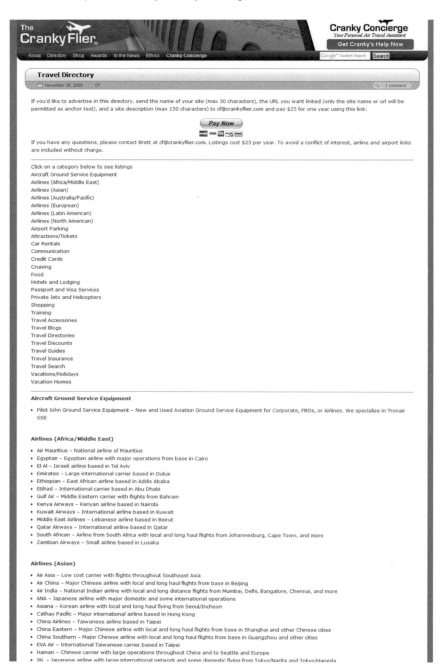

The directory should mirror your topic, but it can be broader. For example, my blog focuses on the airline industry but it's not an airline-specific directory but rather one that broadly focuses on travel. The idea is that anyone interested in airlines might be looking to travel, so this can provide a broad list of companies to help with that process.

The key to a good directory is to make sure there is an order to the madness. If left to their own devices, advertisers will do everything possible to create the ideal anchor text (the text has the link to the advertising website) in order to get the greatest benefit in search engines. The problem with that is if someone wants to use "cheap flights" instead of the name of the company, then the directory is worthless. People who use the directory need to be able to find companies.

So, create several different categories which can hold all potential advertisers. (It's easy to add more later, if needed.) Then set up a structure that has to be followed by all advertisers. Require that only the name or website will be linked and allow for a brief blurb describing what the company does. That's the basis for a good directory.

Sponsorships

Beyond basic advertising there are plenty of options that can be appealing. One of those is sponsorships. Most advertisers want to be mentioned in your content instead of on a sidebar, because they know there's a much higher value to being in a location where everyone coming to the site is focusing instead of acting as a sideshow that might catch someone's eye.

Depending upon how you handle sponsorships, they can provide a way for advertisers to get closer to your content without corrupting it. You can have an official site sponsor that would get mention alongside the name of your site. You can have specific post sponsors that have links around each individual post.

You can also look at having sponsored posts where the content focuses on the sponsor. This can either be a post written by the company, or it can be a post written by you for the company. The latter is generally considered the holy grail of sponsorships. If a company can get you to write a specific post about the company, then it will lend credibility to the company in the eyes of your readers and it will keep the reader focus right on the topic at hand.

If you're going to pursue this type of agreement, be very careful. In order to keep your own credibility intact, you'll need to make sure that it's very clear that the post is sponsored. Otherwise, you have the potential of ruining the trust you've developed with your readers.

That means setting ground rules. Don't write about how you love something if you really don't. If you lie about something and your readers try it, they will be incredibly unhappy with you. That doesn't mean you can't write a sponsored post for something you truly believe in. There's nothing wrong with that, as long as you continue to note that it is sponsored and you are being compensated for it.

Licensing Your Content

An option that can sometimes present itself as a revenue-generating opportunity is content licensing. You'll find that if you write good content, third parties might come to you asking to reproduce the content on their own websites. That's not a bad idea, but you have to be strategic about it.

More often than not, these requests will be made without any pay being offered. If this seems like a bad idea, that's because it almost always is. When people want to get your content for free, that means they hope to make money off it and not pay you a dime. There are a couple exceptions.

In some cases, you'll find that people ask if they can reproduce only an excerpt of your post. To get the full post, the reader has to click through to your site. That's a great type of arrangement, because there's little downside for you. It gives you free distribution to a new set of people, and it continues to bring people back to your site, increasing page views that you can monetize yourself.

I say there's "little" downside, because there is still some. For example, if the site you partner with has a bad reputation as being a spammer or providing bad content, then you won't want to be associated with that site. It may bring you additional readers but it has the potential to hurt your credibility as well. When you're getting started, credibility is very important in helping you develop relationships that can lead to better stories.

Is there any other time that an uncompensated license agreement makes sense for your full content? Yes, and again it has to do with credibility. If you're just starting out and you want to build credibility, you might consider taking a license deal even without pay if it's a site that brings you credibility. Local papers, for example, will sometimes approach bloggers to syndicate their content. If you think this will open doors and allow you to build your standing in the industry, then do it but proceed with caution.

You run the risk of killing your own site in the process. Think about it. If you sign a license agreement, then people might end up going to the other site to read your content. If there's better discussion in the comments at that established site, then people will be more likely to go over there because the discussion is better. You don't want that.

But sometimes you will find license agreements that will pay from legitimate sites that understand the value of your content. These are great ways to expand your readership, increase your credibility, and put a little extra money in your pocket. Just make sure that if you sign up for these types of agreements, you will need to make sure that there is a termination clause that allows you to get out at any time (with a reasonable amount of notice). That's good advice for any contract; you never know if things won't work as well as you hoped.

But content licensing can be a nice way to supplement your existing revenue. It doesn't prevent you from using any other type of revenue model. (If it does, the deal is too onerous.) So it's just a nice extra way to generate some revenue.

Selling Products

Another revenue stream you might want to consider is actually selling products that work with your brand. That can be logo merchandise or just relevant merchandise customers are bound to be interested in. It is incredibly easy these days to sell "stuff" of all kinds thanks to certain sites that offer just in time inventory propositions.

It used to be that to sell products, you would have to make a pretty big commitment. You would have to commission the product to be made, and buy a relatively large quantity. Even something like stickers or buttons could still be relatively costly. The risk was entirely on you. If people wanted to buy your stuff, that's great. But you still had to handle fulfillment of the order: wrapping it up, getting to the post office, and sending it out each time.

Sure, you could streamline that if you had much higher volume, but it's still a cumbersome process regardless. What these newer options allow is for the risk to go completely off your shoulders. The difference? There can be a good-size chunk of a markup on there so it's going to be more costly for your readers to buy something.

You can set up a virtual store with these products and pick and choose whichever ones you like best. You upload your logo and design it virtually. Then you're ready to go.

As mentioned, the problem is it can be more costly for your readers to buy that way. If you find that there's strong demand, you will probably be better off going with the old model of buying in advance and distributing on your own. At least, then you can charge less and sell more.

This is particularly helpful because products can do two things for your bottom line. There is the direct benefit, of course, but there is also the indirect marketing benefit. If someone buys a T-shirt, uses a coffee mug, or sticks a sticker on something, it helps build awareness of your site. Don't be afraid to get downright silly with your ideas to see if it gets a rise out of people. Worst case, nothing sells. But if something catches on, it could provide a nice little side business for you.

Beyond the logo merchandise, there is another type of store that might make sense for you. You can start selling products related to the industry you're covering with your site. Some of these come out as affiliate programs, as we discussed before. For an airline blog, for example, the natural inclination would be to sell airline tickets.

Become an affiliate with an established seller and then you can make money off of each ticket sale. (That's the CPA model at work.)

But an airline blog could also look at selling pilot supplies or travel products. The idea is if someone comes to your site as a reader, you're going to eventually establish good credibility. If you're recommending products or providing assistance in helping people find products that work for them, then you should benefit from an actual sale you help create.

That doesn't mean you should build your own store from scratch, though it's certainly an option. If you think there's a need, you can go ahead and create a store. It might even turn into a storefront at some point and eclipse the blog entirely. But that's a relatively unlikely scenario.

Your best bet is to find a store that already performs the role of selling the materials you want to offer. If you have it, then you can set up an agreement where you'll get a piece of each sale you direct. That can work, but the integration is key.

Don't just slap a link on to your blog and assume the dough will start rolling in the door. If you really believe in what's being sold, you'll want to use advertising slots to entice your readers into buying. This is what was discussed previously under the advertising section. It's a CPA deal, but it's one that fits with the mission of the blog and is something that you really believe in.

It can still be very hard to convince people to buy these types of products, but the more traffic you have, the more you'll be able to sell. It absolutely can become another business line for you.

As you can see, there are many different revenue strategies to be considered, and many of them are compatible with each other. Once you get your revenue strategy in place, you can (and should) tweak early and often to see what works and what doesn't.

Don't be afraid to try new things as long as you think through them properly. If you write about medical supplies, you probably don't want to start doing deals with cigarette manufacturers or alcoholic beverages. If you do something that's appropriate for your site, it's never a big deal if it fails. Just keep trying new ideas and eventually you'll find the right mix to help make the site successful.

Of course, once you find that right mix, don't stop looking for new ideas. Just be respectful of your readers and don't overwhelm them with visual nightmares or confusing situations that might make it harder to enjoy your content.

While it may not seem like something that matters right away, you're going to want to prepare your business structure to include excellent record keeping. This is very important when it comes time to do your taxes. You can, of course, hire an accountant to assist with this but if you're diligent, you can handle it on your own, especially when you're small.

Of course, if you have any questions about what's right for your particular situation, you'll certainly want to contact an accounting professional. Use this as a general guide.

Individual, LLC, or Corporation

As was mentioned previously, there are several different ways to set up your business, and some of it will depend upon how you need it to be structured. In other words, if you're the sole owner, you have a different set of options than if you're going to enter into a partnership with one or more people.

If you're on your own, the most basic type of entity you can use is a sole proprietorship. A sole proprietorship has no legal distinction between you and the business. Any business liabilities are your own liabilities, and you'll pay taxes on all earnings. This is an easy way to set up a business, but there are some disadvantages that we'll discuss when looking at some of the other business types.

If you have more than one person involved in the ownership of the business, then the equivalent of the sole proprietorship is a general partnership. In a general partnership, you have ownership of the company divided up among all the partners. Profits would be split up and taxed as individual income on each partner's personal income tax.

These all sound like a great plans, so why are there even other options? There are a few different reasons why, but often it comes down to liability and taxation.

The issue of liability is why the Limited Liability Company (LLC) was created. This is actually a fairly new business structure and it means somewhat different things in different states, but ultimately it's a hybrid type of company. The big difference between an LLC and a sole proprietorship/corporation is in the name itself—it limits the liability of the owners to include only the assets that are a part of the business.

By shielding owners, LLCs become highly desirable, but there is also a downside. Forming an LLC can take some additional paperwork, and depending upon the state, there may be a variety of different requirements that must be fulfilled.

The beauty of an LLC is that for taxation purposes, it is almost always treated the same way as a sole proprietorship/partnership. LLC members will pay taxes on money that comes in as personal tax but there is no tax on the LLC profits, for the most part.

Some states do require taxation of LLCs in addition to the regular personal income tax that you'll pay. California, for example, charges a flat $800 per year and an additional amount if profits exceed $250,000. In other words, it's a relatively minor tax, but it is still something that has to be paid. Each state has different rules in this regard, so pay close attention to the state in which you live.

You might be tempted to find a state with a favorable LLC law and create your partnership there. Unfortunately, it doesn't work that way. In most cases, if you have business operations in one state, you'll have to pay the taxes there regardless of where you form the company's legal structure.

Chances are that one of these structures will be the best for you as you get started, but there is another type of structure for those with more ambitious plans. That's the corporation.

A corporation is the original way to limit liability for a company, but it's a more cumbersome structure than a simple LLC. Traditional corporations also face double taxation in that corporate profits are taxed as are the dividends paid to members. There are ways around this via different types of corporations (called an S Corporation in the US), but that only makes sense if you feel the need for a corporation in the first place.

The corporation can be particularly useful if the ownership of the company is meant to be separate from the management. That's usually not going to apply to your business, but if it does, you can do additional research on corporations in several different places.

Once you decide on your corporate structure, it will help determine what needs to be done when it comes to record keeping and taxes.

Good Record Keeping

Good record keeping is important for a variety of reasons, some internal and others external. Internally, you want to make sure you are capable of fully understanding where your revenues come from and what costs have an impact on your business. A great deal of insight can be gained by looking into the books of a company, and you'll want access to that insight by keeping good records.

Externally, keeping good records becomes very important for tax purposes. First, you need to determine your taxes, but you also need to support your numbers to the Internal Revenue Service (IRS) if there's ever a question and you have a tax audit.

Good record keeping starts with a general belief that you should record every money-related transaction that impacts your business. This can include everything as follows:

- **Sales**—Any time you make money, you'll want to record it as a sale. This can include advertising sales, subscription sales, product sales, or really anything else that counts as money flowing in. Make sure to categorize each type of sale differently because you'll want to keep track of how your different lines of business are doing.

- **Invoicing**—Sometimes, you'll make a sale at the same time you receive payment. Other times, however, you'll make a sale but payment is due. In those cases you'll want to create invoices to send to your clients. Having invoices with payment due dates make it much easier to keep track of what people owe you and whether or not it's overdue. As part of this, you will also want to keep all of your client contact information readily accessible to make it easy to follow up on payments due. It also makes it easier to identify when former customers have stopped using your service, so you can then market to get them back as clients.

- **Money transfers**—You may have several different bank accounts as previously discussed, which means you'll need to keep track of where your money is at all times. If, for nothing less, to make sure you have enough money in the bank to pay bills. Keep good records and you'll make sure that you never find yourself overdrawn.

- **Bills**—Any time a bill comes in, keep track of it, noting the amount of the bill and when it's due. The last thing you want is to have bills paid late. Your vendors will not be happy and it's not going to help you in your quest to establish your business as a reliable partner.

- **Payments**—As mentioned with money transfers above, you'll want to note every bill payment you make to keep track of how much you have in your accounts.

- **Checks**—Beyond bill payments, you are likely to write checks for a variety of reasons. Keep track of these closely, noting the check number, the amount, and the payee.

- **Credit card charges**—If you do have a credit card you use for the business, keep track of all charges. Make sure to categorize them carefully so that everything is put uniformly into the right categories.

In the end, what you end up with is the ability to go through all of your data and put together trends. If you are able to bring this all together, you'll then be able to look at high-level trends. Which revenue streams are growing? Which ones are not? There are a million questions you can ask, and more important, get answered.

You can also look at cost creep to see which particular charges might be outside the norm. Is there a good reason for the discrepancy or is it something you need to address? The amount of information you can glean from a variety of different reports, the better off you'll be in the long run.

Keeping your eye on the pulse of your business is one of the more difficult things to do when you're stuck in the weeds of day-to-day operations. But take a step back and analyze your finances when you can in order to find how you can improve your standing.

These reports can also, as mentioned previously, help with the IRS. You will be able to put together financial statements (see the next section) and get an accurate picture

Revenue Expense Worksheet

Revenue and Expense Tracking

Sales

       Advertising   _____

       Subscription   _____

       Affiliate   _____

       Donations   _____

Total Sales   _____

Expenses

       Office supplies   _____

       Hosting fees   _____

       Business license   _____

       Business taxes   _____

       Insurance   _____

       Travel expenses   _____

       Meals & entertainment _____

       Dues & subscriptions   _____

       Internet & phone   _____

       Advertising expenses   _____

       Credit card acceptance fees _____

Cranky Flier LLC
PO Box 17982
Long Beach, CA 90807

(888)747-1011
brett@crankyflier.com
crankyflier.com

Invoice

Date	Invoice #
04/29/2012	2001
Terms	Due Date
Net 30	05/29/2012

Bill To

Bob's Advertising Service

Activity	Quantity	Rate	Amount
• January advertising revenue	1	200.00	200.00

	Total	$200.00

of your net business income. If the IRS has any questions, you'll be able to answer them with all the data you have logged over the course of your company's existence.

But just having data alone might not be enough. Keep your bills, payment receipts, and really, any scrap of evidence you can for all of your purchases and payments. You don't need to keep these forever, but you will benefit greatly if you have them for at least a few years after the transaction occurs. There isn't much worse than a tax audit at the hands of the federal government, but it will be far worse if you don't have the documentation to back up your claimed income and, in particular, your expenses.

Cash versus Accrual Accounting

One of the things you'll need to figure out before you can truly keep accurate records is what type of accounting you'll use. Will you use cash accounting or accrual accounting? Let's start with some definitions.

Cash accounting is very simple. When money comes in the door or when it goes out the door, you record it. That may seem pretty straightforward, but let's use an example.

Let's say you sell advertising on your blog for the month of June and you don't require payment until the ad run is done at the end of the month. (This, by the way, is a terrible idea. You should definitely get ad payments up front, but we'll stick with this just to help the story along.)

Chances are that payment will come in during early July (assuming they haven't ditched out on you, laughing all the way, right?). So in a cash-accounting method, even though it applied during the month of June, you wouldn't record it until the money comes in during July.

The same thing goes for expenses. If you were the one paying for that ad on someone else's site, you would record the money going out the door in July even though you reaped the benefit in June.

I think you see where this is going. For **accrual accounting,** you record the payments to the months in which they were applicable, if that makes sense. Let's use a different example that might shed some more light on this.

You've sold a three-month sponsorship on your blog for three million dollars per month (might as well dream big, right?) to Billy's Energy Drink. You sign the deal at the end of December in year one, and payment for all three months comes in the door up front. The term of the sponsorship will be January through March of the upcoming year two.

In the cash accounting method, you would record that nine-million-dollar cash infusion on the books for December in year one. Using the accrual method, however, you would record three million dollars for January, the same for February, and yes, the same for March, all in year two. Not only will the money be shown in different months (December versus January through March), but it's even a different year (year one versus year two.)

Now, the big question is this: Who cares? Why would you pick one over the other? Certainly for a big-ticket sale like this, you'd rather record the revenue in a year where you lost more money because then you would pay less in taxes. But you can't switch back and forth between methods to see what suits you best at the time. You have to pick one and stick with it.

For big businesses, there is no choice. You have to use the accrual method, but this isn't a big business we're talking about. For small business, you have a choice. And most small businesses use the cash method, because it's just plain easier to do. Money comes in, you record it. Money goes out, you record it.

We'll talk about some of the tools you can use to make this whole record-keeping process much easier on yourself later, but first let's dig in a little deeper to talk about financial statements, which ones you need, how to understand them, and why they really matter.

Financial Statements

There are three primary types of financial statements that will be important to understand so you can gauge the health of your business. They are the income statement, the balance sheet, and the cash flow statement.

The income statement gives you a better understanding of your profit or loss during a specific period of time. Public entities are required to publish this information quarterly. While private entities don't have to report, reviewing quarterly statements is still a good standard to use for the business. Still, you can do an income statement for any time period from one day to one decade.

In the income statement, you'll find two basic sides of the equation. First, you add up all of the different types of revenue that you have during that time period. Then you'll add up all the expenses you had during the same time period, and the difference is your profit or loss.

For a sample income statement, see the sidebar on page 78.

Income Statement
Year Ending December 31, 20xx

Revenues

Advertising	$20,143
Sponsorships	$2,000
Subscriptions	$14,999

Total Revenues $37,142

Expenses

Advertising	$1,500
Computer and Internet	$1,000
Consulting	$500
Meals and Entertainment	$483
Office Supplies	$238
Telephone Expense	$987
Travel	$2,483

Total Expenses $7,191

Net Income $29,951

There are other adjustments that have to be made, including interest and taxes, but you get the gist of this. Look at how much money you made and subtract the amount you spent. Voilà. You have a basic understanding of your financial situation. Now, what about the balance sheet?

Unlike the income statement, which is meant to cover a certain period of time, the balance sheet is a snapshot of your business's financial health at a single point in time. Usually, you'll see balance sheets showing the health during the last day of the quarter.

On the balance sheet, there are three components: assets, liabilities, and owner's equity. Let's look at each one of these.

An asset is something that has a positive value and is owned by the company. If you have cash in the bank, for example, that's an asset. If the company bought the

Balance Sheet
December 31, 20xx

Assets
  Current Assets
    Cash $48,035
    Accounts Receivable $2,822
  Total Assets $50,857

Liabilities
  Current Liabilities
    Short Term Debt $1,083
    Accounts Payable $576
    Total Current Liabilities $1,659

  Long Term Liabilities
    Long Term Debt $43,399
    Total Long Term Liabilities $43,399
  Total Liabilities $45,058

Equity
  Owners Equity $5,799
  Total Equity $5,799

  Total Liabilities and Equity $50,857

computer, that's an asset. Even if someone owes you money, that's considered an asset. (It falls under "Accounts Receivable.") The assets stand alone on one side.

A liability is anything that you owe. In the short term, it could be a bill that has been sent to you but you have yet to pay. It could be your credit card bill. (When you do pay it, it will reduce your assets by the amount of cash you send out to pay the bill.) It could be rent. In the longer term, it could be any sort of long-term loan you've taken out to help fund the business.

Think about it this way. If you borrow one hundred thousand dollars to get up and running, that cash will come in the door and become an asset. But you will also have one hundred thousand dollars as a liability to be paid back. Assets minus liabilities will tell you just how much value is in the business.

The thing about the balance sheet is that it has to, well, balance. Since assets and liabilities will not always equal each other, there has to be another component, and that's owner's equity. Assets minus liabilities will equal owner's equity, and that's what you have built up in the business.

What if liabilities are greater than assets? Then you have negative equity, and that's not a good thing. This shouldn't be a surprise to you. (If it is, you might need to go back to an introductory business class.)

Now what about that cash flow statement? What is that good for? It's actually much more useful if you decide to do accrual accounting, because that type of accounting has very little relationship with cash coming in the door (and going out). If you use cash accounting, then a cash flow statement won't be nearly as important. But let's go over it just in case.

Sample Cash Flow Statement

Statement of Cash Flows
Year Ending December 31, 20xx

Operating Activities		
Net Income	$29,951	
Adjustments to Reconcile Income with Cash		
Accounts Receivable	($2,822)	
Accounts Payable	($576)	
Net Cash from Operations		$26,553
Financing Activites		
Loan Proceeds	$20,000	
Net Cash from Financing Activities		$20,000
Net Cash Increase During Period		$46,553
Cash at Beginning of Period		$1,482
Cash at End of Period		$48,035

You may have heard the term that cash is king. This is very true. You might have thousands of dollars in potential sales on the books, but if you run out of money, you can't pay your bills until those sales actually turn into cash on hand. So the cash flow statement strips out all the accounting voodoo and just shows you how much cash came in and much went out.

Cash is so important that you'll need to make sure to keep a close eye on this number. When cash levels get low, you might be in trouble.

That's the basics of financial statements. There are many, many more, but we don't need to get into details on those in this book. The larger your business gets and the more complex your ownership becomes, the more difficult this becomes.

But in this book, we want to stick with the basics, so let's go back and focus on expenses here for a short time. What exactly counts as a legitimate expense?

What You Can Deduct

The beauty of business expenses is that they can help offset your tax bill, when the expenses are legitimate. Think about it. When you make a salary, that money gets taxed by the government regardless of how you spend it. Sure, there are some exceptions—you can write off some medical bills if you have enough of them, for example. But for the most part, the government doesn't care what you buy.

For a business, it's a very different story. Businesses are taxed on net income, which means that your revenues minus your expenses get taxed, not just your total revenues. That's good news but it's not something to be abused.

The IRS will not be kind if you overstep with your deductions. Everything has to be a legitimate business expense. Some of the expenses we discussed before certainly count. Office rent, utilities, computers, web hosting, etc. are all true expenses because they are directly related to your business.

But it can go beyond that. If you have meals with people in order to discuss business, you can deduct that. The same goes for any travel related to the business. Some will be very specific to the type of blogging business. If you write about technology, you can deduct purchases of the tech you use to review or discuss.

This is why it's good to keep separate personal and business finances. It makes it very easy to keep a line between the two sides. But what happens when you use something for both personal and business use?

The most common example, and one that will be of great interest in many a blogging business, is the home office. Can you deduct it? Yes. But you have to be careful.

It's often believed that deducting a home office is a one-way ticket to getting yourself an audit, but it is allowed.

There are a couple of strict rules that must be followed for deducting your home office. First, there has to be "regular and exclusive" use of the space. In other words, you have to use the part of your house that's an office regularly to conduct your business. And that space can't be used for anything else.

If you happen to set up shop in your living room during the day, but then you spend time there with your spouse at night, you can't write it off. But if you have a spare bedroom that is used solely as an office, then you're okay.

The other rule is it has to be your principal place of business. So if you have an office outside the home that is likely your principal place of business. Let's say that you also have an office at home that you use at night and on weekends. That isn't your primary place of business so you can't write it off.

Another split use that you're likely to encounter is your car. For the most part, you'll only be able to deduct the percentage of the car that you use for business based on the miles that you drive. There is also a per-mile amount you can deduct for when you're driving on business. This can be tough to keep track of. For example, if you go to an interview then stop at the supermarket on the way home, can you write that off?

You will have to use your best judgment when you determine how many miles you drive for business and how many miles you drive for personal use.

Beyond this, there are a few other things that can be deducted. For example, taxes you pay for the business are deductible. Interest expenses are deductible as well. Don't forget any sort of training you do to help you become a better blogger. That's right, buying this book should be a perfectly legitimate, deductible expense since it's directly related to your business.

Do You Need Accounting Software?

If this is all starting to make your head spin, there's a good reason for that. It should be straightforward, but you'll be amazed at how complex it becomes in short order. You're probably going to want to get accounting software to keep this all under control.

One of the most popular types of accounting software is QuickBooks, by Intuit. There are, however, many others that can achieve the same thing for you.

List of Accounting Software Providers

There are many different ways you can keep track of your expenses from a piece of paper to an Excel spreadsheet. For those who are looking for some outside help to keep everything in order, here are some accounting software providers:

- Quicken (www.quicken.com) is meant primarily for personal users, but you can use it for basic businesses either online or with the desktop version.

- QuickBooks (www.quickbooks.com) is from the same people as Quicken but it's a full-fledged business accounting program available online or in a desktop version (where you have the software on your computer).

- Outright (www.outright.com) is a simple online alternative to QuickBooks for basic accounting purposes that doesn't include invoicing (you can use Freshbooks for that).

- WaveAccounting (www.waveaccounting.com) is a free online accounting option with invoicing.

- WorkingPoint (www.workingpoint.com) is another online accounting option with invoicing as well.

Traditional accounting software is installed on your computer, but over the last few years, there has been a big shift to cloud-based options. You can now sign up for services stored entirely online. That will enable you to access it anywhere you can access the Internet instead of having it sit only on one machine.

Security is always a concern for this type of shift, but a great deal of work has been done to make sure your data will be secure. Still, it's something that you will need to consider when you decide what solution is right for you.

The best part of all these systems is they can help you with your taxes as well. With desktop products, you can print all the data you need to pass to an accountant, if you use one. With online solutions, you can even give access to your accountant so she can access all of your data with ease.

How Long to Keep Documents

Once your system is in place, you'll start accumulating records quickly. Fortunately, when things are held electronically it makes it easy to keep them forever as data storage gets cheaper every year.

But what about paper records? How long should you keep those? You'll still accumulate a fair number of them, including receipts for business expenses, and it's important to hang on to those as proof, especially if the IRS decides to audit you at some point down the line.

Fortunately, the IRS issues guidelines on how long you should keep your records. In general, it's a good idea to keep records for three years after the tax year in which you filed, but there are some documents that you might want to keep indefinitely.

According to the IRS, the key is to keep documents until the period of limitations is up. That's the point at which you can no longer amend your return. Here are the periods of limitations straight from the IRS:

1. You owe additional tax and situations (2), (3), and (4), below, do not apply to you; keep records for 3 years.
2. You do not report income that you should report, and it is more than 25 percent of the gross income shown on your return; keep records for six years.
3. You file a fraudulent return; keep records indefinitely.
4. You do not file a return; keep records indefinitely.
5. You file a claim for credit or refund after you file your return; keep records for three years from the date you filed your original return or two years from the date you paid the tax, whichever is later.
6. You file a claim for a loss from worthless securities or bad debt deduction; keep records for seven years.
7. Keep all employment tax records for at least four years after the date that the tax becomes due or is paid, whichever is later.

09

Legal and Ethical Issues

When it comes to blogging, two of the biggest concerns should be legal and ethical issues. Bloggers fall into a gray area where it's unclear if they're considered to be journalists or not. It can even vary by state. But legal issues have the ability to sink you and your blog very quickly. Ethical issues can do just as much damage, though for different reasons. This might seem like more of an extraneous topic, but it's not. This is actually quite central to the success of your blogging business. Take note of everything below and use it as a reference going forward as you continue to build your business, because it will be incredibly important at some point down the line.

Terms of Use

When you're setting up your website, you should consider creating Terms of Use along with a Privacy Policy. This will make it clear to all of your readers exactly what they can expect from your blog. This doesn't seem like it should be necessary, but we live in a litigious society so it can never hurt to go above and beyond to really make sure that you've been completely clear.

The Terms of Use simply states what readers are agreeing to by reading your site. This doesn't require any proactive action on the part of the reader, but you should make the link clearly available on all pages for easy access.

Most of what goes into a Terms of Use is legal mumbo jumbo. But it can help protect you in case of a lawsuit. Whether or not it's frivolous, this can only help your case. In short, you basically want to explain that the site is for informational purposes only, you can't guarantee accuracy, you have no responsibility for what happens on another site if someone clicks a link from yours, and the user understands all of this.

I have included the "Terms of Use" for The Cranky Flier below. You'll want to do more research on your own to make sure that you have something that fits your site directly, but this can help point you in the right direction.

The Cranky Flier Terms of Use

Use of this website/blog is offered to you on your acceptance of these Terms of Use, our Privacy Policy and other notices posted on this website. Your use of this website or of any content presented in any and all areas of the website indicates your acknowledgment and agreement to these Terms of Use, our Privacy Policy and other notices posted on this website. If you do not agree to be bound by and comply with all of the foregoing, you may not access the website. The Cranky Flier (CrankyFlier.com) has the right, at its sole discretion, to modify, add, or remove any terms or conditions of these Terms of Use without notice or liability to you. Any changes to these Terms of Use shall be effective immediately following the posting of such changes on this website. This website is for informational purposes only and is not intended to provide specific commercial, financial, investment, accounting, tax, or legal advice. It is provided to you solely for your own personal, non-commercial use. You may link to and refer to this website freely.

This website does not guarantee the accuracy of any information. Accordingly, we do not guarantee the accuracy, timeliness, reliability, or completeness of any of the information contained on, downloaded, or accessed from this website.

The performance of this website and all information contained on, downloaded or accessed from, this website are provided to you on an "as is" basis, without warranties of any kind whatsoever, including any implied warranties or warranties of merchantability, fitness for a particular purpose, or non-infringement of the rights of third parties.

We reserve the right to modify, disable access to, or discontinue, temporarily or permanently, any part or all of this website or any information contained thereon without liability or notice to you.

As a visitor to our website, you acknowledge and agree that any reliance on or use by you of any information available on this website shall be entirely at your own risk. In no event shall The Cranky Flier nor any of its data providers be liable for any direct, indirect, consequential, or exemplary damages arising from the use or the performance of this website.

Confidentiality and Transmissions over the Internet

The transmission of data or information (including communications by e-mail) over the Internet or other publicly accessible networks is not secure, and is subject to possible loss, interception, or alteration while in transit. Accordingly, we do not assume any liability for any damage you may experience or costs you may incur as a result of any transmissions over the Internet or other publicly accessible networks, such as transmissions involving the exchange of e-mail with us (including those which may contain your personal information). We make no efforts to safeguard the privacy of the information you provide us. All submissions to this website via e-mail or otherwise becomes our property. In no event will the information you provide to us be deemed to be confidential, create any fiduciary obligations to you on our part, or result in any liability to you on our part in the event that such information is inadvertently released by us or accessed by third parties without our consent.

User Conduct and Obligations

You agree to follow all applicable laws and regulations when using this website and further agree that you will not transmit junk mail, chain letters, or other unsolicited bulk e-mail or duplicative messages to any e-mail address listed on this site. You also agree to not submit spam to the site comment system.

By uploading, posting, or otherwise transmitting through or to our website any content, you grant to us, our successors and assigns, a nonexclusive, worldwide, royalty free, perpetual, non-revocable license to use or distribute such content in any manner that is compliant with our Privacy Policy.

Indemnification by User

You agree to indemnify, defend, and hold us and our friends, spouses, children, and agents harmless from any loss, liability, claim, demand, damage, or expense (including any legal fees) asserted by any third party relating in any way to your use of this website or breach of these Terms of Use. We reserve the right to assume the exclusive defense and control of any matter subject to indemnification by you, which shall not excuse your indemnity obligations.

Third Parties and Links

Links or pointers to other websites and references to products and services offered by third parties are provided to you for convenience only and do not constitute an endorsement or approval by us of (i) the organizations that operate such websites; (ii) the content, privacy policies, or other terms of use on such websites; or (iii) such third-party products and services. As we have no control or responsibility over websites or content maintained by other organizations, or for products and services offered by third parties, we do not assume any liability for your use of any of the foregoing, which use you acknowledge and agree shall be at your own risk.

Please note that Cranky Flier LLC has financial relationships with some of the merchants mentioned here. Cranky Flier LLC may be compensated if consumers choose to utilize the links located throughout the content on this site and generate sales for the said merchant.

Proprietary Rights

Our policy is to comply with all intellectual property laws and to act quickly upon receiving any notice of claimed infringement. If you believe that your work has been reproduced on this website in a manner that constitutes copyright infringement, please let us know immediately by sending e-mail to cf [at] crankyflier.com and the work in question will be removed.

General

If any provision of these Terms of Use is held invalid or unenforceable in any respect by any court having competent jurisdiction, such provision shall be enforced to the maximum extent permitted by law, and the remaining provisions of these Terms of Use shall continue in full force and effect. No waiver of any provision of these Terms of Use shall be deemed a further or continuing waiver of such provision or any other provision of these Terms of Use.

These Terms of Use shall be governed by and construed in accordance with the laws of the State of California and the laws of the United States of America. The parties consent to the exclusive jurisdiction at a place to be determined by The Cranky Flier.

Accepting Free Products and Services

Once you have the legal stuff nailed down, it's time to start thinking about ethics. Some people get into the blogging game because they want free stuff. As bloggers become more prominent, they will get more and more offers to try out a product, use a service, take a trip, etc. The temptation is certainly there to take everything that comes in the door and enjoy it, but that's a bad idea.

It's not that accepting free products and services is a bad idea in itself, but without a strict policy on how to handle it, you could end up doing some serious damage to your reputation. In the blogging world, your reputation is really all you have. If people don't believe that you're writing truthfully and that you're on somebody's payroll, then you aren't going to gain much traction for a sustained period of time.

Some people may not care about a reputation and are simply looking to make a quick buck. There are people out there who create blogs, work their magic to drum up traffic, make money, then shut it down and move on to the next once people catch on to the scheme. If that's what you're looking for, then this isn't the right book for you. This book is about creating a long-term, sustainable business. And that business is built in having a solid reputation.

As stated, that doesn't mean you shouldn't accept anything for free or for a discount. The likelihood is that many of the things that would be of interest to your readers might be out of your financial reach. If you have an opportunity to leverage your blog in order to provide a better experience for your readers, you should. But to make sure you do it right, you must make sure that you are adequately disclosing your relationships.

Disclosure to Your Readers

The biggest mistake that bloggers make is to not disclose that something has been given to them. Secrets are bound to sink your site, because your readers will be naturally inquisitive. Why would you keep a relationship secret at all? You might get more money and more opportunities. Some brands think that if it looks like an authentic review on a blog, then they will get more mojo from that. The problem is that if you're exposed, then you'll both look terrible. The brand will probably survive, but that might be the end of your site.

So what's the right way to do this? Be completely up front about it. Early on, when I started my site, I created a Code of Ethics (see page 90). At the time, the concept seemed foreign to a lot of people, but I have received a great deal of

Code of Ethics Template

Ethics is a hot topic in the blogging world these days, so I've decided to put my code of ethics front and center. You'll see the code below along with all sorts of disclosures. My goal is to be an open book here. You can always contact me with questions or comments at xx@yy.zz.

Code of Ethics

For the purpose of this code, "free and/or discounted products and services" refers to anything offered to me for free or for a discount simply because of my status as a blogger.

- When I write about free and/or discounted products and services, I will always disclose on this page who gave them to me, when they were given to me, and when I wrote about them. I will also include the discount amount offered in any post on the products/services.

- I will always write the truth about a product or service regardless of whether it is good or bad. I will never trade favorable press for free and/or discounted products and services.

- I will only accept free and/or discounted products and services if the people offering the product/service confirm that they have read this code of ethics and are willing to abide by the rules that have been set here.

- Just because I have been provided with free and/or discounted products and services doesn't mean I will write about them. The only criteria for determining whether or not to write about a product are if it will make for a compelling post, good or bad.

List of Offered Free or Discounted Products/Services

The following is a full and complete list of products/services that have been offered to me along with whether or not they were accepted. This list does not include invitations to events unless a free or discounted product or service accompanied that invitation. (I apologize if I missed something small from the early days of the blog. Let me know if I need to add something.)

Company	Offer	Date	Accepted	Blogged
XYZ Corp	Dinner with executives	03/12/2011	Yes	03/16/2012

Additional Disclosures

- I am currently being paid to write a weekly column for xxx.

- I currently have no equity holdings in any companies about which I write.

Historical Disclosures

- My consulting work for zzz ended in August 2012.

praise from readers and other bloggers alike. In fact, several other bloggers have asked if they could copy my policy for their own site. That's the best thing that can happen.

The Code of Ethics serves two purposes. It informs the readers, of course, but it also makes it clear how you operate to those companies that are interested in working with you. And that can be equally important in helping to establish credibility. Many of the more respected brands appreciate such an open and honest policy since some bloggers have been known to try to take advantage of brands to further their own needs.

That's why one of the most important pieces of the Code of Ethics is that you will require all brands to have read the policy before you accept anything for free or at a discount. This ensures that there is no miscommunication about how you handle these situations. If a brand comes back to you afterward with complaints you can point to the Code of Ethics informing them that they knew exactly what they were getting into. I also suggest requiring the brands to ask you before sending anything. There's no good reason for a brand to send you something if you don't think it will be interesting.

The cornerstone of the Code of Ethics is to state that you will not trade good press for free or discounted goods and services. You will always write the truth, if you decide to write at all. And that's another piece of the policy. Just because something is offered for free doesn't mean it will be written about. As you become more prominent, the offers for freebies will increase dramatically. Sometimes, you might think something will be good to write about, but in the end it turns out that it's not. That shouldn't be an issue, so make it clear up front.

If you do write, it might be a glowing review or it might be a terrible one. More likely than not, it's something in between. This is easy to say in advance, but you need to make sure to stick with it in practice. If brands are smart they will try to provide you with the best experience possible, but things can go wrong, and they need to realize that if that happens you will write about it.

The final key piece of the policy is disclosure. Though I wouldn't bother to disclose little things like a holiday card sent by a company, I would strongly suggest disclosing anything significant that's been provided. If possible, write the date it was offered, exactly what was offered, and link to the post or posts where you wrote about it. This can help the reader to identify exactly what's happened and when.

I also make sure to disclose any relationships that might have a potential conflict. If you own stock in a company, write it down. If you do any consulting or freelancing work, write that down. You can't over-disclose for these types of things, so anything that might be considered a potential conflict, even remotely, should be disclosed.

This doesn't even have to be current. If you have past disclosures, then put it down. You can even link to resumes and/or biographies so you have a complete detailed history of yourself and others who write for you. It helps people to get a complete understanding of how you might have been influenced in the past, even if it's subconsciously. Be an open book in that regard, and you really can't go wrong.

Always try to think about things from the perspective of a reader. If you were reading another blog, then how would you feel if you found someone was getting something for free but not disclosing it? Just do what you would want to see in other sites and then you will be successful.

But it's not just about ethics in terms of accepting freebies. There's also an ethical and legal question about how you cite your sources and use your images in posts.

Plagiarism and Sources

One of the worst things you can do as blogger is to steal content. I'm not talking about physically stealing a product or service, but rather stealing thoughts and ideas. Most people know this as plagiarism, which is defined by Merriam-Webster as "to steal and pass off (the ideas or words of another) as one's own: use (another's production) without crediting the source." The problem is there is no bright line as to what constitutes plagiarism and what constitutes an original work. It's a gray area, and that means you can get into trouble if you aren't careful.

The clearest example of plagiarism is simply copying and pasting the exact thoughts and words from another source and passing it off as your own. This should never be done, ever. If you want to incorporate thoughts from another source, feel free to do so, but make sure that you've quoted it and accurately cited the original source. Since this is a blog, you should always try to link directly to the source from within the post if you can. Help your readers explore these thoughts in greater detail by handing them off to the sources you find to be so valuable. Don't be afraid of losing your readers by including links. You're only helping them find good information, and that will keep them coming back.

Sometimes, you can get direct quotes from sources by interviewing them and that should always be cited properly as well. Use the name and title as your source wants. (Of course, if your source wants to remain anonymous, then you need to decide if that's something you want to do or not. But of course, make sure it's clear that the thought is coming from someone else and not from you.)

Where plagiarism becomes difficult to discern is when you yourself aren't aware that you're doing it. That may sound strange, but consider how many conversations you likely have with people about the topic at hand. Those conversations help to mold your thoughts, and so you might end up using the thoughts of others in your writings without even realizing it.

I'm not trying to scare you here, but it is a very serious subject. Be incredibly careful with how you use content, and do everything you can to make sure that it's original. If it's not, you better be citing it properly. You can't, however, just take any content you want and paste it into your site. There is something called Fair Use (see page 94), and you should never use more than what's appropriate. Content from other sources should be used to provide you with something to comment on. It should be supporting material and not primary material, unless you have the explicit permission of the content's original author.

Using Images

In case you were wondering, images are considered content, and you can't just use images at will unless you have the permission of the original author. Fortunately, there is a vehicle for images to be put out there with permission without having to have any interaction with the author. This all depends upon the license being used.

It's highly recommended that you use images to help improve the readability of your posts. Large blocks of text can be tough to swallow for a lot of readers. Images

Fair Use

The concept of fair use is a simple one but it is not well defined. Whenever an original work is created (at least in the US and most of the developed world), there is a copyright on that work that belongs to the creator of the work (or someone/something else if the copyright has been assigned). It means that to use that work in your new work, you need to get permission, and that could include royalty payments.

There is an exception to this and that's where "Fair Use" comes into play. This was codified into law under 17 USC § 107 - LIMITATIONS ON EXCLUSIVE RIGHTS: FAIR USE as follows.

> *Notwithstanding the provisions of sections 106 and 106A, the fair use of a copyrighted work, including such use by reproduction in copies or phonorecords or by any other means specified by that section, for purposes such as criticism, comment, news reporting, teaching (including multiple copies for classroom use), scholarship, or research, is not an infringement of copyright. In determining whether the use made of a work in any particular case is a fair use the factors to be considered shall include—*
>
> *(1) the purpose and character of the use, including whether such use is of a commercial nature or is for nonprofit educational purposes;*
>
> *(2) the nature of the copyrighted work;*
>
> *(3) the amount and substantiality of the portion used in relation to the copyrighted work as a whole; and*
>
> *(4) the effect of the use upon the potential market for or value of the copyrighted work.*
>
> *The fact that a work is unpublished shall not itself bar a finding of fair use if such finding is made upon consideration of all the above factors.*

Not very clear, is it? The point is this: You can use a snippet from another piece of copyrighted work without needing permission if you are using it for your discussion. So you can point to another source and use a one line quote if you want to comment directly on it. You should always cite where the information came from, and you should never use large chunks of the work. (There is no set definition on how much you can use, but just use the very small, very pertinent pieces.)

can be funny, educational, or just basically background. You can decide what's best for your particular blog, but just having images will be helpful in your quest to generate more traffic.

Where can you get these images? The easiest option is to take them yourself. If you're reporting on something, make sure you have a camera with you. Take lots of pictures and you can obviously use those as you see fit since you took them. Of course, that's not always possible. You'll want to find other ways to supplement your images.

Public Domain

The first option is to look for images that have been released into the public domain. The rules can vary by country, so be sure to look this up to make sure that you're complying with the law. In the United States, works in the public domain generally include any images that have had their copyrights expire or works that have been specifically released into the public domain for a variety of reasons.

In general, works that have had their copyrights expire aren't going to be of much use. Sure, if you're looking for things in the distant past, they might have some value, but if your focus is on current newsworthy items, that won't work. A great source of public domain material is the United States government. In fact, any government assets within the US are entered into the public domain, so you can use government images quickly.

If an item is in the public domain, there is no requirement that you get permission to use it, and you don't even have to attribute the work to the original author. It is generally recommended, however, that you include the citation, if you know it. It's just good practice, even though it's not required.

Licensed Photos

Fortunately, asking for permission can be a lot easier thanks to specific licenses. In these instances all you need to do to use an image is obey the guidelines. The most popular licensing scheme for this is called Creative Commons (www.creativecommons.org.)

Creative Commons was designed to allow people to upload their photos and attach a specific license to that photo. Large photo sharing sites like Flickr.com specifically allow people to attach a Creative Commons license to their images. This makes it very easy to obtain permission—it's built into the license.

A great source for finding Creative Commons content is on the website itself at http://search.creativecommons.org. This will allow you to search multiple websites for content that is specifically licensed to be used by others.

What is Public Domain?

The concept of work being in the public domain may be a bit confusing. Anything that is in the public domain means that it is free of copyright and can be used without citation or permission by anyone. How does something get into the public domain in the US?

- Anything created by the US government that is publicly available is in the public domain

- Any works that have seen their copyright expire are in the public domain. Since 1978, copyrights in the US have expired 70 years after the death of the creator. For work where the copyright is not assigned to a single person, the copyright expires either 95 years from publication or 120 years from creation of the work, whichever is less.

Generally, if something is really, really old, it's in the public domain. This very famous painting (see above), for example, was created before copyrights existed. But if someone made changes to the painting and put his own spin on it, that work would be copyrighted.

You can find a list of resources to identify public domain materials at: http://en.wikipedia.org/wiki/Wikipedia:Public_domain_image_resources

Within Creative Commons, however, there are actually six different types of licenses. So you'll need to make sure that the image you want is licensed properly. Even if the image isn't directly going to be used for e-commerce, you should still get an image that allows commercial use. You are, after all, trying to build a business here. Then you'll need to decide for what you want to use the image.

If you're planning on making any changes to the image before you use it on your site, then you'll need to make sure that the license for that image allows for modification. Some artists will allow you to use their image, but only if you leave it as is. So be sure to double check before using an image.

Then it's just a matter of noting how you need to cite the image creator and how you need to share the image.

If you find an image, you might think the best way to include that on your website is to link off to the image on the original website and have it called up every time your site loads. That is the opposite of what you should do. Many sites have limitations on bandwidth, and if you send a lot of traffic to someone else's site, you're going to slow them down or even cause them to crash. The only time you should use an image directly off another website is if that website includes a link to embed. Flickr.com, for example, is built for this purpose so you can just grab the embed code and put it in your site. On most sites, however, that's not a good thing.

For most sites, just save the image and upload it to your own server. (You'll be able to do this through your blog software.) Or if you prefer to use a third-party host for your images, upload there.

Third-Party Hosts

There are many places you can store your photos on the web, including many places you probably already use, like Facebook. Once you have your photos stored somewhere on the internet, you can embed them on your blog. Here are some sites to review.

- Facebook: www.facebook.com
- Flickr: www.flickr.com
- ImageShack: www.imageshack.us
- Imgur: www.imgur.com
- Picasa: www.picasa.google.com
- SmugMug: www.smugmug.com

When you do, make sure to check the license. Some Creative Commons images require that you also share the image with the same license. They call it Share Alike. If that's the case, you can't take a Creative Commons image, modify it, and upload it with a copyright. It has to be shared the same way as the original.

All Creative Commons images will have specific instructions on how they want to be cited. In fact, when you click through on the license, the HTML code will be presented so that you can just copy and paste how you cite it.

Stock Images

There is one other option for images, and it can be good in certain cases. You can always pay for an image. There are plenty of sites out there that sell stock images for use on your site. This is the kind of thing that might be good in certain situations if you can't find the image you need using other methods, but it's a very expensive way to do business if you run a blog. This is generally useful for something that generates a significant amount of revenue, needs high quality images, and isn't very frequent.

This is the best way to get perfectly clean images—without the blemishes you find on the regular amateur photos you'll find for free online. But professional-quality images do cost a fair bit, so you aren't going to be able to afford many of them.

Sites like istockphoto.com run on a credit system. You can buy as little as six credits for $9.75 (for $1.63 a credit) all the way up to 30,000 credits for $31,200 ($1.04 a credit). Then you can use those credits to buy images on the site. For many of these, you're looking at five credits just for an extra small image. It goes up quickly from there. So as you can see, this is very expensive for a daily blog. Where I've found this type of image helpful is for bigger, more permanent images. For example, it might be helpful to pay for an image when you're designing your logo since that should look as good as possible.

Liability—Is Libel an Issue?

You've probably heard about libel and slander, and you'll want to make sure that you never participate in either. With a blog, avoiding slander is easy since it requires defamation orally. Since you're a writer, this isn't a big concern. But libel is an issue, and it's something that you need to pay close attention to.

In short, libel is when you publish something (words or images) that you present as fact but are not. If that does harm to the subject, then he or she (or it) can sue you

Stock Image Sites

If you want to use stock images, here are some sites that will help you find them:

- Dreamstime: www.dreamstime.com
- Getty Images: www.gettyimages.com
- iStockphoto: www.istockphoto.com
- Jupiter Images: www.jupiterimages.com
- Shutterstock: www.shutterstock.com

Once you're on these sites, you might be a little confused about the different types of licenses. Here are some of the more common types of licenses:

- **Royalty free:** You pay a flat fee that allows you to use the image in multiple instances. You will need to check the specific license for details, but you have more flexibility here. This license is nonexclusive, meaning others may end up using the same photo.
- **Rights managed:** You pay a fee that entitles you to use the image once. If you want to use it again, you have to purchase another license. With this, you can sometimes get an exclusive license meaning that you will be the only one allowed to use that image, but it will be costly to do so.
- **Subscription:** This type of license allows you to pay a fee per period of time and it entitles you to use a certain number of images while you are subscribed.

for damages, and you'll be out of lot of dough. When you're in the business of digging up information and publishing it, this is a very real problem.

The best defense against a libel claim is to tell the truth. If you publish something shocking and scandalous, you're going to have some very angry subjects. But if it's true, you are protected. Just make sure that if you make a factual statement, you can back it up.

For example, let's say you accuse an airline of flying aircraft in unsafe condition. Do you have maintenance records that show deficiency? Was there a fine from the government citing conditions that were found to be unsafe? If so, then you should absolutely publish that. But what if you're just going on hearsay from someone in the company? That person could be disgruntled. It wouldn't be the first time that incorrect information was fed from within the company in order to hurt one's employer.

If you publish that information, the airline might decide to come after you. You better be ready to show that you can back up your claim with facts. Even if you didn't have the facts originally but you can find them and present them when the claim is made, that still proves you were telling the truth.

But telling the truth isn't the only test for claims of libel. There also has to be harm done. Going back to our example, if you claim an airline is unsafe, there is undoubtedly going to be backlash. People might book away from that airline, and the airline will be able to quantify it. There was real harm done, which means you could be on the hook for those damages if your claim proved not to be true.

What if you had claimed that a charity had wasted one million dollars for overhead in a year when in fact it was two million? Technically, that's not a factual statement, but there were no damages. In fact, the one-million-dollar claim was less damaging than the truth of two million dollars so there would be no libel claim here.

There is one last hurdle before libel can truly be claimed, and that's that you didn't do enough legwork to prove the level of truth. Let's say that you went ahead and did all sorts of research. You found documents that proved to show deficiency and you had several witnesses and sources. What if those documents ended up being forged and you were duped? In that case, there would probably some sort of criminal case against the person who forged those documents. This, however, would be a defense you could use to show that you did your due diligence to ensure that the claims you made were correct. It would be up to the judge to decide, but there is a level of work out there that should excuse you from a libel claim.

Opinion versus Fact

One thing that you can do to protect yourself is to state something as an opinion rather than a fact. Now, if you say that it's your opinion that an airline is flying unsafe airplanes will that get you off the hook? It might not. It probably wouldn't prevent the airline from trying to take some sort of action against you. Even if you win the case, you'll still have to deal with lawyer fees and the tremendous amount of time wasted on the case. But if you say it's your opinion that management isn't spending enough time monitoring aircraft maintenance, then that's a fair statement. It's not a factual statement at all, but it is just showing your opinion. You're allowed to have an opinion.

Unfortunately, in the US, nothing prevents someone or some entity from filing a lawsuit that's not for valid reasons. These can often be filed in order to try to shut down a site from disseminating news with the hope that the site will not have pockets as deep as the entity. In that case, the site will have to stop publishing this information just to make the lawsuit go away in order to save money.

This has been termed a SLAPP, or Strategic Lawsuit Against Public Participation. In these lawsuits, the plaintiff generally doesn't go into it thinking that he or it can win. Instead, it's just an effort to silence critics by trying to drain financial resources.

In these types of cases, it can be possible to win legal fees back but that still requires fronting the fees in the first place, a luxury many people and companies can't handle for lengthy periods of time. The wheels of justice turn slowly, which means there can be real pressure.

Finding a Lawyer

The only way to avoid a lawsuit ever is to stop writing. But since you want to have a blogging business, that's not going to be an option. Instead, just make sure you're incredibly careful about what you write and how you phrase it. There are plenty of resources out there that can help you specifically in this area. In addition, make sure that you have access to legal resources. Find a lawyer who can help you if you get into trouble.

Really, the best advice is to find a lawyer who can help you before you begin writing. Get help in setting up your company and in learning the best practices. Find someone for your staff who is familiar with these types of legal issues and can help in an editorial capacity when it comes to reviewing posts.

Ultimately, you may have to decide the tone you want to use when writing. How hard-hitting do you want to be? Sometimes, the best way to get page views is to go with a sensational headline or by twisting the truth. We've seen this happen in media since the word *media* was invented. But you might need to leverage that with your willingness to fight a lawsuit. What's the best tone for your site to have? Make sure you consider potential legal ramifications when you make that decision.

There is one other thing that you need to think about: whether or not you're actually a journalist. That might sound like a funny question, but it has big ramifications. Unfortunately, the answer to that question isn't entirely clear at this point.

Are You a Journalist?

As a blogger it may seem unimportant to ask whether or not you're considered a journalist. After all, it's sort of a hybrid medium that allows anyone to become a citizen journalist. But if you are trying to put together a legitimate blogging site, then you would think that journalistic protection would apply.

What is journalistic protection? In the US it's commonly known as shield law. Shield laws give journalists the right to keep their sources private. This is essential for any news-gathering organization. If you can't keep your sources private, people won't talk to you. Or if you promise to keep your sources private and are forced to divulge them, you can be in even more hot water with those sources.

There is no federal shield law, but about 80 percent of states have one in place in order to provide protection to journalists who are doing important work. The difficulty arises in determining who is actually protected by these laws.

In Oregon, for example, only people employed by official media outlets can receive that level of protection. This came to light in court when a blogger was deemed by a federal judge not to be a member of the media. If she was, then under Oregon law, she'd be able to post a retraction for a story she wrote that was incorrect. Only if she refused would she be open to a defamation lawsuit. Since the courts found that she was not a member of the media, she now has a $2.5-million judgment against her for defamation.

For most bloggers, this kind of thing will never happen, but it depends upon the subject at hand. If you're writing about Beanie Babies, you're probably not going to have a problem. But if you get into politics, especially local politics, then you may become highly visible and susceptible to lawsuits. This becomes even more likely if you use a more controversial or aggressive style, as was the case in Oregon.

Just make sure to keep all of this in mind when you're thinking about how you write about a subject and what information you want to use. It is always important to maintain journalistic integrity if you hope to establish any level of credibility. For that reason, any sort of false accusations could prove to be quite harmful to your reputation as well as to your pocketbook.

Copyright

Let's turn the tables here for a second. Instead of thinking about reasons why you could be sued, let's talk about reasons why you might want to go after others. It sounds strange, since you're the one exposing yourself online and not the other way around, but there are some reasons why you might want to consider taking some action.

The biggest reason by far is copyright infringement. Some people believe that you have to actually register in order to be protected by copyright laws, but that's not true. Anything you write is under copyright unless you decide to release it. You don't even have to submit a notice of copyright, but it is still recommended. You've probably seen this before: "© 2012 John Doe" or something like that, right? Put that on your website and put the dates of publication. It can't hurt, and it serves as notice that the work is copyrighted.

It should be noted that the author of the work holds the copyright unless stated otherwise. That's why if you have employees writing for you, it should be noted in their contracts that the work they produce is work for hire. The same should be done even if you use freelancers or part-time writers. Your lawyer can help you draft the proper language to ensure that your business holds the copyright.

How long does your work stay under copyright? When an author holds a copyright, it is valid for the life of the author plus seventy years. When it comes to works for hire, then it is valid for ninety-five years from the date of publication or 120 years

Registered Copyright Benefits

You might be wondering why to bother registering your copyright. The government recommends registering your copyright for the following reasons. These are directly from www.copyright.gov:

- Many choose to register their works because they wish to have the facts of their copyright on the public record and have a certificate of registration.
- Registered works may be eligible for statutory damages and attorney's fees in successful litigation.
- If registration occurs within five years of publication, it is considered prima facie evidence in a court of law.

As you can see, the main reason for registering your copyright is that it makes it easier to enforce if someone violates it.

from the date of creation, whichever is longer. In other words, you have nothing to worry about.

Should you register your copyright even if you don't have to? That's something you need to decide for yourself. There are some protections afforded to registered works that might be useful for you. The most important of these is the right to sue.

If you need to sue for copyright infringement, you need to have registered your copyright with the federal government. Some will suggest that you should register it no matter what just so that you have the added protection, but others will point out that if you can't imagine yourself suing for copyright infringement, then it's not worth bothering.

The reality is that registering your copyright is fairly simple. In fact, it can be done online at copyright.gov. Just log on and you can register your works for a nominal fee. There is one problem, however. How do you register a work that is constantly changing?

You update your blog several times per week with new posts, so can that be registered before you even write the content? No, it can't. For sites that are frequently updated, the general recommendation is to file an updated copyright registration every three months, that is, if you plan on registering.

Let's say you want to register. Here's how you do it: Once your site is created and your first post is made, go ahead and visit copyright.gov to file your registration. You will first need to create a free account then you can create a filing for your blog. Online submissions cost thirty-five dollars as of the time of publication, and you can pay with a credit card or bank account.

You will need to submit a "deposit" of your work. If your site has little to no content, you can submit the entire thing. Otherwise, you will need to submit five representative pages of your work as produced. Once that's done, the registration is noted.

Three months later, you can file another registration. You don't just include the new work but you file all work that you have created so far. This is then filed as a derivative work. In other words, you're really just updating your existing registration with new information.

Why do this every three months? Why not daily? Why not once a year? The reason to not do it daily is obvious. The idea of having to pay thirty-five dollars every single time you create a new post is crazy. Not only is it a lot of money it's actually quite a waste of money as well.

There is a three-month grace period on filing your copyrighted material. That means that if you write something today, you can still register it for up to three months. In other words, if you file once every three months, then your work will be protected at all times.

Finding Copyright Infringement

Let's get back to the original point of registering your copyright in the first place. It's done in order to protect your work in case of copyright infringement. Copyright infringement is when a person or entity takes your work without your permission and reproduces it. This is bad for a number of reasons. It can end up taking traffic away from your site. It can help others earn revenue off your content without sharing any of the profits. It can also give someone else credibility if that person received credit for taking your work. In short, it's a bad thing.

Even though we spoke at length about copyright registration, there are plenty of things that you can do without actually registering your content. The first thing you will want to do is set up alerts that monitor for your content.

This is easier said than done, but there are some things you can do. For example, go to Google and set up Alerts for your name, your blog name, your web address, or anything else that's likely to be used frequently in your posts. Often, you will find that automated sites will just take everything and repost it.

This doesn't help if your name and any identifiable marks have been removed from the content. For that, it's more difficult to follow. There are services that will actively monitor for copyright infringement, but you will likely not be interested in those until you become much bigger and copyright infringement becomes such a big threat.

You can also do random search in Google and other search engines to see if key phrases of your content pop up on other websites. But this sort of manual process is not likely something you are going to want to do very often. Still, the biggest offenders tend to repeatedly steal your content, so a random check every so often will help.

Once you've found an offender, then what?

Fighting Copyright Infringement

You've been browsing the Internet and you came upon someone stealing your content. How do you deal with it? First, make sure that it's a legitimate theft. At one point, you may have signed a content license agreement of some sort or another. Make sure this isn't just a related website, because you don't want to waste your time chasing down offenders.

Also, make sure that it really is all of your content being stolen. There are some aggregator sites that take snippets of content and then link back to your site for the full story. This generally falls under fair use, if there isn't an overly large chunk of content being used. You might actually like this because it has the potential to send traffic back to your site.

But let's assume that you have found a real offender and you want to take action. The first step is to see if you can find contact information for this website. Often, sites that are stealing your content are in the business of trying to make a quick buck. They're hoping to get higher ranking in search engines and eventually, turn that into a money-making opportunity. Because of this, they go through websites like nothing. They often won't have contact information of any sort, so it can be hard to find.

When that happens, you can try to look up their contact information via WHOIS. (There are several places to do this, but www.whois.net works well.) When websites are registered, it is required that contact information be provided for each registrant. Sometimes, privacy is enabled, but there should still be a contact at the host that you can contact with your complaint.

The cease-and-desist letter sounds fancy, but it's a pretty simple document. You are simply requesting that the other party stop copying your content (cease) and never do it again (desist). Lawyers will be happy to help you with the creation of one of these letters, but you can find plenty of templates online if you'd prefer to do it yourself.

You might be surprised to see that this kind of letter does get a response. Most people won't bother sending these types of letters, so often people on the other side will just walk away and find some other content to steal where they will encounter less resistance. Other times, however, the letter will just be ignored.

When that happens, there are other avenues you can consider that don't involve legal action. The best option is to file a Digital Millennium Copyright Act (DMCA) takedown notice. This is a notice that requests that the offending copy be removed immediately. The difference with a DMCA notice, however, is that you aren't asking the offender. You go straight to a more powerful source.

You can send a DMCA notice to the web host directly. As mentioned above, you can find the web host by looking up the information in WHOIS. Send the DMCA notice to the web host and it should comply with your request if it is valid. How easy this is can depend upon the web host you're dealing with, but often that will get you a better response than you'll get directly from the offender.

Here is an example cease and desist letter that I have used.

Dear Sir or Madam:

You are republishing the content of the website The Cranky Flier, http://www.crankyflier.com, in its entirety, including all text and images, without consent or compensation of the original author. This is a violation of The Cranky Flier copyright, and you are hereby notified to cease and desist immediately.

Proof:
http://xxxx.info/category/the-cranky-flyer/
duplicates the entire copyrighted content of
http://www.crankyflier.com/

This is unacceptable and illegal. A previous friendly notice requesting that you discontinue the publication of this content on xxxx was not only ignored but it has now spread to another site. That has forced us to take further action.

You may either: 1) use a short excerpt of the post, to be understood as "fair use" of the copyrighted content; 2) arrange for a resyndication contract permitting full-feed republication, with financial terms to be discussed separately, by contacting the editor, Brett Snyder, at cf@crankyflier.com; or 3) remove The Cranky Flier content entirely from your site, including all archived posts.

Please note that your copyright infringement also violates your terms and agreement with Google Analytics and any affiliate partners you represent on your site. In various forms, each of these partners prohibits the violation of intellectual property or proprietary rights of third parties. If you fail to adapt your site's use of The Cranky Flier, we will contact your advertising partners to notify them of your violation.

DMCA violation notices will also be submitted to your web hosting company and domain registrar.

If we do not receive confirmation of your agreement to the terms laid out above, we will proceed with DMCA takedown notices at 12 noon, Pacific Standard Time, Friday, February 3, 2012.

Your prompt attention is appreciated.

Sincerely,
Brett Snyder
CrankyFlier.com
cf@crankyflier.com

You can also file this request directly with search engines. Many times, the content is stolen because the offender is trying to draw more traffic in to the site and monetize it. (You come to their site, you click on the links, and they make money.) One way to stifle that is to file your complaint directly with the big search engines. Google is the biggest, so it's best to start there. Go to http://support.google.com/bin/static.py?hl=en&ts=1114905&page=ts.cs and you can file your complaint there. If you have the content removed from searches, that significantly hurts the thief's ability to make money off your content. When that happens, they're less likely to bother stealing it.

Trademark Registration

I'm sure you're sick of talking about registering things with the federal government, but here's one more for you to consider. Your copyright is the content of your work, but there's also the trademark to consider. What is that? Your trademark is your unique identifier that separates your business from others. Quite literally, it's the mark that you use in trade. You will also hear about a service mark. While a trademark is used relating to goods, a service mark is the same thing relating to services. You will generally hear them referred to collectively as a trademark regardless of the actual application. In this case, it should be the name of your blog.

As with copyright, you do not need to actually register your trademark to have it. You simply need to use it in the course of business and be the first to do so. That's right. You can't just create something and start calling it Coca-Cola. Unless you've been living under a rock, you know that mark has been used for over a century, though there actually is a way you could use it in a limited sense. We'll get to that later.

That means the hardest part of this whole process is simply finding a mark that hasn't already been used. You probably have some sense of what has been used and what hasn't since you've already looked with your state to see if the name of your entity has been taken. You also had to choose the URL for your website. That helps.

But it doesn't mean that your name hasn't been used by someone somewhere else. The best way to find out is to search at the US Patent and Trademark Office at www.uspto.gov. This is another area where an attorney can really help make the search a smoother process, but you can navigate it on your own.

The first step is to use the TESS link (Trademark Electronic Search System) you can find on the US Patent and Trademark Office website. It will let you do a basic search for your mark. Start very narrow to see if there's a match but then quickly broaden your scope. When I first went to register The Cranky Flier, I started with a search for just that. But then I expanded it and searched for anything with the word "Cranky" in it. That brought a lot more results, but it helped me to be sure that my trademark had not already been used.

Now, remember when I said you could potentially use Coca-Cola even though it's already been registered? That's because when you register a trademark, you have to declare what goods and services are actually being marketed. Without a doubt, Coca-Cola has registered its trademark for beverages, but it has also done it for just about everything you can imagine from napkins to lip balm. Good luck finding something you would like to use it for that isn't already in use.

But with lesser known brands, you can find times where the offerings are so different that you can coexist with the same mark. Just make sure to look at what goods and services are registered.

I mentioned before that you don't have to register your trademark and that is true, but it does help if you take the steps to do it. As with copyright, you can't take legal action unless you've registered the mark. In addition, by registering it, you're staking a very public claim to it.

Once you receive the mark, you no longer write your name as NAME™. Instead, it becomes NAME®. That may not seem to be important, but it gives an air of legitimacy.

If you are confident that there is not going to be any sort of conflict between your mark and another, you can begin the filing process. For a trademark, you only need to file once, and you might be surprised to find that you can include images in your trademark. I've found it most useful to just stick to the title in order to keep it simple, but you can also register how you display your name. Just keep in mind that you have to pay an additional amount for every mark you file and every category you use with goods and services.

You can file online for the mark using the TEAS link (Trademark Electronic Application System), again on the US Patent and Trademark Office website. Please note that obtaining a mark is not a fast process. Once you file your application, it will be reviewed by the office to make sure everything is complete. (If you don't feel comfortable getting to that point, you really might want to consider an attorney.) Eventually, it will be published so that anyone who might have an objection has the opportunity to see it.

If there are no objections, then this process can be completed within a year. With any complications, it can stretch easily into a multiyear process. Be prepared for delays. Do remember, however, that you can continue to use your mark even before the process is complete. The only reason to stop using your mark is if you find yourself in violation of someone else's registered trademark.

10

Growing Your Audience

If you're coming to this point in the book, that hopefully means that your business is up and running and you're happy with how it's going. With the infrastructure in place and everything moving along well, it's time to start thinking about growing the business.

Once your business is up and running, the infrastructure is in place, everything is moving along well, and you're happy with how it's going, it's time to start thinking about growing the business. The best way to grow the business is to grow your audience. The way to catch the attention of advertisers and sponsors is to get a big, targeted audience. The bigger and more relevant the audience is to the advertiser, the more they'll start drooling over your site. Here are some tips on growing.

Sharing with E-mail and Feeds

One of the easiest things you can do is provide as many options as possible for people to read your site. No. 1, of course, is just posting the blog. That way, people can come directly to the site and read what's being said. But that's really just a start.

Some people don't like to actively go to blogs where they have to "pull" information themselves. Instead, you can set up methods that will allow you to "push" the information directly to them. The easiest way to accomplish this is with your RSS feeds.

RSS stands for Really Simple Syndication and it's made for just that. An RSS feed puts your content into a stripped-down file that makes it easy to communicate the data to other places. Whatever blogging platform you choose will make RSS feeds available to you. Just look around on the platform's help pages to find the address.

Complying with the CAN-SPAM Act

The US government's CAN-SPAM Act protects people from e-mail spam at the hand of business. Since you will likely be using e-mail as part of your business, here is what you need to know to comply. If you don't, you risk thousands of dollars in fines. This is directly from the Bureau of Consumer Protection in the Federal Trade Commission:

1. **Don't use false or misleading header information.** Your "From," "To," "Reply-To," and routing information—including the originating domain name and e-mail address—must be accurate and identify the person or business who initiated the message.
2. **Don't use deceptive subject lines.** The subject line must accurately reflect the content of the message.
3. **Identify the message as an ad.** The law gives you a lot of leeway in how to do this, but you must disclose clearly and conspicuously that your message is an advertisement.
4. **Tell recipients where you're located.** Your message must include your valid physical postal address. This can be your current street address, a post office box you've registered with the US Postal Service, or a private mailbox you've registered with a commercial mail receiving agency established under Postal Service regulations.
5. **Tell recipients how to opt out of receiving future e-mail from you.** Your message must include a clear and conspicuous explanation of how the recipient can opt out of getting e-mail from you in the future. Craft the notice in a way that's easy for an ordinary person to recognize, read, and understand. Creative use of type size, color, and location can improve clarity. Give a return e-mail address or another easy Internet-based way to allow people to communicate their choice to you. You may create a menu to allow a recipient to opt out of certain types of messages, but you must include the option to stop all commercial messages from you. Make sure your spam filter doesn't block these opt-out requests.

6. **Honor opt-out requests promptly.** Any opt-out mechanism you offer must be able to process opt-out requests for at least 30 days after you send your message. You must honor a recipient's opt-out request within 10 business days. You can't charge a fee, require the recipient to give you any personally identifying information beyond an e-mail address, or make the recipient take any step other than sending a reply e-mail or visiting a single page on an Internet website as a condition for honoring an opt-out request. Once people have told you they don't want to receive more messages from you, you can't sell or transfer their e-mail addresses, even in the form of a mailing list. The only exception is that you may transfer the addresses to a company you've hired to help you comply with the CAN-SPAM Act.

7. **Monitor what others are doing on your behalf.** The law makes clear that even if you hire another company to handle your e-mail marketing, you can't contract away your legal responsibility to comply with the law. Both the company whose product is promoted in the message and the company that actually sends the message may be held legally responsible.

For more, go to www.business.ftc.gov/documents/bus61-can-spam-act-compliance-guide-business.

The most obvious application for something like this is e-mail. If people don't want to come to your website, then you can allow them to sign up for an e-mail subscription. You can set it up so that your subscribers will receive an e-mail either at set time intervals or whenever you post something new.

A quick warning on this. If you start trying to manage this yourself, be careful. There are rules about e-mail spam that you must follow strictly. See page 112 regarding the CAN-SPAM Act.

This really isn't something you should have to worry about, at least not initially. You're going to be way too busy working on other parts of the business, so you're better off letting someone else manage this process. Not only is that easier, but there are free services, like Google's FeedBurner (www.feedburner.google.com), that will take the entire process off your plate. In FeedBurner, you just set up which feeds you need and then you can set up the timing interval as well. FeedBurner provides you with links or text boxes you can add to your site so people can sign up, and it does the rest.

The downside to one of these services is that you don't have complete control over the look and feel of the e-mail. Initially, that shouldn't be as big of a problem, but in the long run, you might want to make a change to a paid service with more customization. That's something you can worry about down the line, but you shouldn't have to deal with an expense along those lines this early in the process. You need to focus on the content in the beginning.

Another thing to consider is exactly what you want to send via e-mail. That's right, you don't just have to do posts. You can set this up for comments or even for specific blog categories. While setting this up for posts is the most important, you will also want to keep your ear to the ground to see if there's demand for others. We'll talk about comments shortly.

The RSS feed is actually good for more than just sending e-mails. Though some have proclaimed this to be an old and soon-to-be dead technology, there are still a sizeable number of people who follow blogs through RSS-feed readers.

Some of these feed readers you might use every day and not even realize that you can add your own content this way. My Yahoo!, for example, is a portal that many people use as their home page. You can add your own content to this page by including any RSS feed and it will show up. This is something many of your readers might prefer to do if they already visit My Yahoo! every time they load their web browser.

There are also dedicated feed readers people use to aggregate all of their feeds in one place. Google Reader is just one of the many options for feed readers, and it is free. On these sites, you add all the RSS feeds you want from all the different sites you read so that you only have to go to one place.

For both of these options, the key is making your RSS feed readily available to any and all visitors to your blog. When you choose the theme for your blog, most will include a link to the RSS feed already. You can always move it around or add more links to additional feeds for comments, categories, etc. if you'd like.

Remember, offering as many feeds as possible doesn't hurt you or your site in any way. It takes very little time to set up, and the benefits can be great. The bulk of people will subscribe to either the main posts feed or the comments feed, but that doesn't mean you should stop there. Some people might be interested in a particular company, or a specific location, or a certain type of post (like technology for example). It makes sense to try to cater to these people by making feeds available for them.

I've found it easiest to create a new page with a link to all the feeds you've created. Put the links to the most important ones on every page on the site, but go ahead and link to an extra page that has every other link there. It may not get you a tremendous amount of traffic, but it certainly won't hurt. Providing choice is always a good idea when you want people to read your site.

Social Media

There are other very obvious ways to share your content with people, but it's worth separating these from the previous ones. With feed readers and e-mail, it's more about delivering the content to a single person than about pushing it into the world of social media. Sharing your information via social media is all about trying to get others to share the information and join in the conversation. That should be a key strategy in trying to grow your audience.

As mentioned earlier in the book, the current eight-hundred-pound gorilla is Facebook, and without question you should be sharing your posts there. But how should you go about doing it? The simplest way is to link to a post every time you write something directly from your Facebook account. You can do this manually if you want to leave a comment yourself or you can even automate it so you don't even need to think twice.

There are sites out there that allow you to automatically post on social media sites every time something new comes up. Check out http://dlvr.it and http://ifttt.com to see a couple of examples of how you can set that up. This works with multiple social media outlets, so you can set it up and forget about it.

But should you do more than just post a link? That is something you need to consider on your own. There are plenty of social media outlets out there and you simply can't participate in all of them. Remember when everyone had to be on Friendster? Then it was Myspace. Nobody bothers with those anymore, and that's generally the way the web works. Something gains traction quickly and then falls away when something better comes along. But that doesn't mean you should avoid social media at all. It just means you should pick and choose how you want to participate.

Posting via Facebook

Facebook is great simply because it's where so many people are today. The potential reach is tremendous, and it doesn't look like there's anything that's going to pose a real challenge to Facebook yet. You need to be here in some form, even if it is just sharing your posts from your personal account.

If you want, you can create a Facebook page for your site. Many people will tell you this is essential, but ultimately it's only essential if you're going to make use of it. An active Facebook page is going to get a much better response than one that you set up and then ignore. In fact, a dormant Facebook page will probably send the wrong message to people who stumble upon it.

Facebook is good for sharing links and having conversations. If you're going to create a strong presence, you'll need to participate in them without just promoting your own posts. The time commitment can end up being a lot greater than you originally anticipated. Before you decide to jump into Facebook, do some experimenting and make sure that you can adequately participate to get the most of out it.

Tweeting

If you're talking about Facebook, then Twitter can't be far behind. With its short bursts of text (no more than 140 characters), Twitter lends itself well to sharing articles and having short comments. I've also found Twitter to be really good for connecting with your readers without having to spend a great deal of time on the relationship.

Twitter is the most "real-time" of the tools out there. In other words, when someone sends a tweet with a question, they expect a response in a much shorter amount of time than they do if they send an e-mail. So if you want to open yourself up to being on Twitter, you should be prepared to monitor it and respond in a timely fashion. Otherwise, you're likely to simply frustrate your readers. This is an art, not a science. In other words, there isn't a set amount of time that you're given to respond. There's also no firm standard on which tweets should receive responses. You'll just have to feel it out and create your own personality as you go with Twitter.

What you will find with Twitter is that it can be a great tool for discovery. Beyond just seeing trends and getting ideas for posts, you can really start to connect with people virtually. Find people who write influential blogs in your space. Look for people who work in the industry or people who use the product. When you follow them, you'll be able to see what's on their minds. As a bonus, people will often (but not always) follow you back if you follow them. That opens a window for you to get them to check out your site. Don't immediately jump at the opportunity to do that, however. Enter into conversations, comment on what others say, and answer questions if you can help people. You don't need to spam people with links to your blog over and over again. If they start to like what you say, they will find it.

This then leads to the next question. What if someone follows you? Should you follow them back? There are a lot of different beliefs about this. Some say it's proper etiquette to return the favor, but I disagree. Only follow those people who you actually want to follow. If you end up following too many people, then you just end up losing the most important ones in all the noise.

You can follow people as a courtesy if you'd like, but you will end up doing that with the express intention of not paying attention to what they say. Some will still say this is polite, but that's for you to decide. If you do that, you will need to set up lists in Twitter that you can follow. That helps you elevate those that you really want to follow to a position where you'll see what they say.

Still, as I mentioned, I'm a fan of only following the accounts that interest me. As I write this, I follow only 184 people even though I have more than 85,000 followers.

Posting via LinkedIn

Another tool to consider using to promote your site is LinkedIn. This is particularly helpful for industry-specific blogs, and it's really helpful if you already have a strong network. Since you connect to people you know for business purposes, you can reach a highly targeted market via LinkedIn. That can mean something as simple as automatically putting up links to your posts for all to see. It can also mean joining groups that have active conversations about the topics featured in your blog. Providing great comments in that setting can really help build your credibility and ultimately get people to come to your site.

If this sounds difficult, it's not necessarily. There are some great, free tools out there to make following all of your social media networks fairly easy to do. Take a look at Seesmic.com, for example, or Tweetcaster.com, which is now owned by Twitter itself. These types of tools can really help bring a sense of sanity to the fast-paced world of social media by organizing your conversations and helping you identify what's important.

Encouraging Conversations (Comments)

There is one other type of conversation to focus on, and it's the comment section. You can't underestimate how important an active comment section can be to building traffic on your site.

When it comes to blogging, you should be looking to get people actively involved in your site. It's that kind of involvement that ends up breeding loyalty. If people comment, they'll not only be there to read your post, but they'll keep coming back to read additional comments. I've had posts where the comments themselves were far more interesting to read than the post. That's a great thing.

When people comment, they feel a much greater passion toward the topic. It gives them both the ability to express themselves and a sense of ownership in what you're building on your site. In other words, it gets people more excited about what you're doing because they're a part of it.

That's why you should make commenting as easy as possible. It's why I don't recommend requiring people to sign up for an account in order to comment, and it's why I don't recommend moderating comments. Encourage the free-flowing conversation and you're bound to see a benefit.

Part of this means making it easy for people to know when comments have been posted. We already talked about RSS feeds, and those should without question be incorporated into your site. You can have comment feeds that let people see comments flow in as they're posted. You can even set up an RSS feed for each individual post if you'd like.

What I've found to be most effective, however, is just a simple e-mail link. When someone posts a comment, they can sign up to have an e-mail sent every time an additional comment is posted. If you're using WordPress, for example, there is a plug-in called Subscribe to Comments that will do just that. Other systems have other methods for implementing this sort of notification. It is essential that you have it set up so that people who are already invested in the conversation can continue to be notified when new information is posted.

Friends and Family

There's been a lot of discussion so far about strategies for getting better participation on the site, but there is one that's incredibly simple we've left out: Reach out to family and friends to get help. Some of this can be accomplished via social media tools like Facebook, where you're probably linked to your friends already. But you can be more aggressive by directly asking friends and family for support than you probably would by just posting something on a social network.

Your friends and family will be eager to help you build up your new business, because that's what friends and family are for. They're there to support you when you need them, and starting a new business is a great time to ask for their help.

It can be as simple as sending an e-mail to your friends to ask them to visit your site. You can also ask if they know anyone else who would be interested. Even ask if they would comment on your post on a social network or help comment on the blog as well to spark conversation. You might even want to think about having business cards printed to give them. If they meet someone who they think would be interested in your site, they can just hand over the card. You might not think that this would happen a lot, but it does. And your friends will be there to help if they can.

Feel free to do things like ask for feedback on your posts. They'll be more likely to give you honest feedback.

Introduction to Fellow Bloggers

One thing you might want to consider is finding a way to become a part of the blogging community in your particular area of discussion. There is no set community in that you get a membership card and meet up for monthly drinks or anything like that (though I suppose there could be in some industries), but that type of mentality does start to build over time.

As we discussed earlier, there are many different possible niches in each industry, and that means that some blogs might be more complementary than competitive to you. But even the ones that are competitive should be viewed as competitive in a good way.

When it comes to blogging, your readers are looking for quality information in well-written format. If someone else provides that, it doesn't prevent readers from visiting both that site and yours. Assuming you aren't charging for your content, the only constraint for a reader is time. You just need to make sure your content is worth the time it takes to read. If there are other blogs in the space, that may make it more competitive for someone's time, but if you all provide worthy content, readers will make time.

One way to do that is to get into back and forth discussions with other bloggers on your sites. If you see someone write something that piques your interest on another site, talk about it on yours. This could be something you agree with completely and think it's worth sharing or it could be something that you completely disagree with and want to poke holes in. Either way, you might feel it worthwhile for comment.

These types of things have a way of growing into something bigger. When you link to another blog, a pingback is nearly always received by that site. On some sites, you'll see it posted in the comments section when someone else links to that post. The good news about this is it provides a link to your site but more important, it lets the other blogger know that you've been writing about something he or she said. This might trigger a response from that side, and it can turn into a very interesting discussion for bloggers and readers alike. You don't have to limit yourself to this kind of interaction, however. You can even get into a strong back and forth via social media tools like Twitter or Facebook regarding a post.

I'll give you a great example from personal experience: I write about the airline industry, but I'm not a so-called "points blogger." This is a group of people who focus on earning and redeeming miles and points in the various frequent-flier programs out there. Personally, I consider myself miles agnostic and don't really care who I earn points on. That has led to some interesting back and forth interactions over the years between sites. Having such different opinions can make for truly compelling reading.

But there are other ways to help ingratiate yourself into the blogging community. First and foremost, read their blogs. Learn which blogs you like most, and then actively comment on them. Become a fan, participate in the discussion on those blogs. If you feel like you have something to say, start reaching out via contact links on the site. Don't be a pest, but if there's a contact link, it's there for a reason. They want to hear from readers just as you will with your site.

One of the most common types of e-mails I see is the link exchange request. I hate these. New bloggers will often send me a note saying that they love my blog and would love to exchange links in my blogroll.

A blogroll is a standard feature on most blogs that is basically a list of sites that are recommended by that blog. This is a highly desirable list for two reasons: One, it can help readers of that site find your site (since your sites are likely similar, this would be a great way to gain new readers); second, it helps with search engines when you get a link. I'll talk about that below.

For some, this list becomes a tool for trying to extort links out of other sites. E-mails often begin with "If you add me to your blogroll, I'll add you to mine." I refuse to participate in these types of things and you should too. What you put in your blogroll is your list of personal recommendations. People follow those links expecting quality, so you shouldn't just exchange a link with anyone who asks. You risk sending your readers to sites you don't actually like.

Instead, craft your blogroll to link to sites that you really like and recommend. If you want, you can send an e-mail to that blog to let them know that you have linked to them. You might even explain that you're not asking for a link exchange, because you don't work that way. You would certainly appreciate a link to your site, but that's not the point of your e-mail. Thank them for doing good work and move on. That will get a much better reception than just a link exchange request, which may very well simply be thrown into the trash.

I mentioned this before, but I'll say it again for extra emphasis: Read the blogs you respect and actively comment on them. Join that community and put some extra effort into it. The blogger will likely notice, and it might spark him or her to visit your site just to see what you're writing. At the very least, if you leave intelligent, thoughtful comments, you'll be able to develop a solid reputation for yourself.

Finding the Right Forums

Don't just limit yourself to commenting on blogs, however. Make sure that you become a part of the broader community as well by looking for the local e-watering holes. Before the Internet, people used to gather together in person to talk shop. You still see that today, but the Internet allows for broader, more frequent discussion from passionate individuals on your particular topic.

Some of these forums are just casual online discussion groups that you can join. You can find these on places like LinkedIn, as mentioned previously, and you can find them through places like Yahoo! Groups and Google Groups. That can be great for spreading the word about your site, but more important, it can help you get great content to write about. If it's an open group, then the information should be public and you can write about it. If you're concerned, you can always ask.

You might find some groups that are closed, and you can get invited in by others. Those groups are generally only for tight-knit groups, and you won't be able to write about what comes directly from them, but they can help form your opinions. They can also be a lot of fun.

Those types of groups, however, will require getting an invitation, usually from someone you know. It may come over time, but it's not something you can really force. What you can do, however, is participate in the broader sites.

Beyond the smaller discussion groups, there are bound to be other sites that are the big places where people gather to talk about your industry. These might be enthusiast sites or they could be for investors. They could also be for those in the business or for frequent users of the business. No matter what, they will be good places for you to monitor what's happening in the industry and to participate in the discussion.

Many of these people will be the influencers around the industry in one way or another, so you'll want to definitely find your way into being a part of the group. But this isn't the only way to meet influencers.

Attending Conferences

An easy way to start meeting people and building your network is at industry conferences. Most of these are open to anyone, though it might cost you some money to get in the door. Depending upon the conference, many will actually offer media passes if you're planning on covering the show for your blog. Your blog will, of course, have to be relevant or they won't bother. Others will only give passes to larger media outlets, so in the beginning, you might just have to pay to get in the door.

Think very carefully about what type of conferences you might want to attend, because even if admission is free they can be expensive to attend. You'll need to get yourself there, assuming it's not in your home town. And then you'll need a hotel, transportation, and you'll want a budget for food and drink. So unless the conference is in your town, make sure you do your homework to see if the right people will be at these shows.

If you're trying to attract people in the industry to read your blog, then go to conferences that are meant to appeal to those who work in your industry. But what part of your industry matters to you? If you expect to get manufacturing folks to read your blog, then go to their conferences. If it's more of a sales and marketing thing, go to theirs. There are a lot of different types of conferences, and only a few will probably make sense, depending upon how wide you cast your net as a blogger.

If you write about more consumer-facing issues, then the net will be cast even wider. You'll be interested in getting industry folks to read your blog, but you also want to start developing them as sources you can use for stories. You'll also want to think about consumer-facing shows as well because those are your prime readers. This is difficult if we're talking about low-dollar products because everyone could be a customer. If it's a specialized product that's either high priced or has limited interest, then you might be able to find a good show worth attending.

Exhibiting at a Conference

Should you think about exhibiting at a show like that? Probably not. It's usually fairly expensive to exhibit at a show, and the benefit is minimal for a small blog just starting out. It could make some sense at a consumer-facing show in low-dollar industries, because then there might be tremendous foot traffic, but it will still probably be too difficult to justify the high price.

Find the Right Conference

All of this talk about different kinds of conferences really brings up the next big question: How do you find the right conferences to attend? The best way is to ask people. Presumably, you have some level of experience and exposure within your industry. That means you're going to have friends in the business as well. Talk to them in order to learn which conferences matter. Which ones should you attend?

Another factor will be finding out which conferences you actually can attend. Every conference will have a website, so be sure to check it out. While many of the larger conferences are open to anyone who wants to pay, there are exclusive conferences that require you to get invited. If the conference was recommended by a friend, maybe he or she can get you on the list.

You'll also need to figure out which conferences you can afford to attend. As I mentioned, some will give you complimentary admission if you're part of the media, but that's not always going to be the case. For example, in the travel industry, PhoCusWright is one of the big business-to-business conferences each year. But PhoCusWright now has a strict blogger policy that has turned off many bloggers from covering the event. PhoCusWright will only hand-pick bloggers it deems worthy of attending. And for the privilege, bloggers are required to pay one thousand dollars. Once accepted, bloggers are expected to tweet "consistently," post photos and videos, and post about the blog highlights. While the need to limit the number of bloggers is understood, these requirements have pushed many to simply avoid the conference.

But this is an outlier. For many conferences, you'll have a good chance of obtaining a free pass if you write about topics relevant to the show itself. Some conferences may disqualify you because of your size or newness, but it's always worth trying to gain access. The worst thing that happens is you're told you can't get a free pass. You can't lose anything by trying if you don't find an official policy in place on the conference website already.

Let's say you have an unlimited budget and you're ready to tackle the conference circuit by storm. Do you really want to do that? There are so many different conferences out there that if you attended every one, you could probably be permanently on the road, hopping from frozen big conference center to frozen big conference center. You wouldn't even know the day of the week. This might be a decent strategy in some instances, but in general, it will just burn you out. So find the conferences that are best.

In general, you'll want to find a conference that has an active tradeshow floor. Most will have educational sessions/speeches of some sort as well as a tradeshow floor for people to wander and learn more about each company. At some conferences, the tradeshow floor traffic is heavy, and you can meet a lot of people that way.

At other conferences, most of the meetings are arranged before arrival at the show and they're all done behind the scenes. This is great if you know people and can arrange meetings in advance, but it's terrible if you want to wander the floor and meet new people. All of the movers and shakers will be behind closed doors. So find a show that has a good, active tradeshow floor.

If you're looking to grow your network and meet people in the industry, a smaller conference will often be a better bet than a big one. You would think that a big one would provide more opportunity, but at those shows, people are usually very busy and use their limited time for important meetings. You aren't going to make that cut, at least not in the beginning.

At smaller shows, there can be more flexibility. After all, each person has the same amount of time in a day, but there are fewer things that need to be done during that time if it's a smaller group. Consider that as you work to figure out which shows to fit into your schedule.

Arranging Speaking Engagements

There is another great way to decide which events are the best for you, and that involves trying to reach out for speaking engagements. In the beginning, you'll be lucky to be invited, and you may have to pay your own way beyond admission to the show itself, but it will get you great visibility.

It's not like anyone can just walk up and be a speaker, however. It takes a lot of effort to cultivate relationships and build your reputation. This isn't going to happen overnight, no matter how badly you think it might.

Conference organizers look for a few different things when it comes to building their roster of speakers. One thing they like is, of course, a big name. I've seen larger conferences bring people like former President Bill Clinton in to speak even though it may not be directly related to the conference itself. Big names bring big audiences. This isn't you, or at least it won't be, for many, many years.

Other than that, conferences like people who are very knowledgeable about the subject at hand and who tend to be opinionated and outspoken about the topic. Bloggers can be great for these types of engagements, because it's our job to be outspoken and knowledgeable about a topic. Of course, doing this on paper doesn't mean that you'll be good at it in a spoken form.

Are You a Confident Public Speaker?

Before you even start to think about trying to get a speaking engagement, make sure you'll be up to the task. Do you have a good speaking voice? Can you articulate your thoughts? Are you comfortable being on stage?

A lot of writers find out quickly that while they're great on paper, they hate getting up in front of crowds. If you can overcome that fear, more power to you, but for some, it's too powerful. When you get up on a stage, you need to be able to perform. The whole reason for doing it is to establish your credibility in the industry and get more people to know your name. If you get up there and bomb, you aren't going to make any headway in your quest.

If you aren't sure you have the right speaking personality for this kind of thing, go to a friend who you know will tell you the truth. It shouldn't be hard to find out if you can do this well or not.

Types of Speaking Engagements

If you decide you can do it, you then need to know what different types of engagements there are. There are the single speaking opportunities, where you stand up and deliver a speech to the crowd on your own. Those are usually prepared speeches with questions at the end, at times. There are also panel discussions, where you would just be one participant on a panel with multiple opinions. These may very well start with a prepared opening bit by each person, but it will usually turn into a moderated discussion.

These types of engagements are very different. With a speech, it's all about preparation. You need to be able to write the speech and then put together a strong delivery. With a panel discussion, it's more about knowing your topic and being able to think quickly on your feet. Each of these require very different skill sets, so you'll want to think about that before you dive in and try to participate.

If you think you're up to the task, you just have to start finding out about potential opportunities. You'll certainly want to start with smaller conferences or potentially with smaller break-out forums at bigger conferences. If you know the conference organizers, then that's your best bet. Talk to them, let them know that you're interested in speaking. If they're your friends, you can certainly be blunt about it. With any luck, you'll be able to get a spot on a panel, because that's far more likely than getting a starring role giving a speech.

If you don't know anyone who puts these things together, just keep attending conferences and meeting people. Eventually, if you have the right personality, you will probably find your way on to a panel one way or another.

Once you get on your first panel, you'll know how well you can handle these kinds of things. You might find you get a rush from doing it and you want to do a lot more. You may get the opposite feeling as well—you might find you hate it and simply don't want to ever do it again.

If you can do it at all, then you really should. It's a great way to build your brand and increase your credibility around the industry. And that's going to be tremendously helpful as you look to build the blog and your audience up to something greater.

Become a Source

I realize that you already have a very long list of things to do when it comes to building up the blog, but here's one more thing to consider: Try to become a media source yourself.

This might sound kind of funny, because you're actually turning the tables on yourself as media, but it's yet another great way to build an audience. And this is actually something you can start to accomplish fairly quickly.

When I first started blogging, I was amazed at how early reporters from newspapers or other journalistic outlets started asking me for quotes for articles. Now, this wasn't the *New York Times* or the *Wall Street Journal* calling right off the bat, but it was smaller outlets.

It turns out that many reporters search for information on stories the same way most of us do; they head to Google and start searching. The difference is that while most people stop when they find the information they need, a reporter will seek out the author of the story in order to try to get a quote.

That's what I found happened in the early days, and you will probably find the same thing. Once your blog starts popping up in Google search results (something we'll talk about shortly), then you can instantly become a potential source for someone who is looking for comment on a topic you've written about previously.

Depending upon the industry about which you're writing, there might not be very many good sources of independent information out there. My specialty is the airline industry, and that's a very crowded industry when it comes to media coverage. But even within that crowded industry, there were some topics that hadn't been tackled very much, and that opened a door. If your industry is even less covered than that, you'll have an even easier time starting to build yourself up as an authority on the topic.

If you write about issues important to a certain locality, those local news sources might be the first to find you for a comment on a certain topic. If you talk about things more broadly, you aren't going to be limited. Any local media sources from anywhere could contact you if they're doing a story. The local news sources are likely to be your best bets at first, because they are looking for a local angle from a local commenter.

This can extend beyond just newspapers. There are magazines, trade publications, local TV news, and more. Once you do find yourself being used as a source, make sure to tout it for others to see. Create a media or news page on your website where people can see where you've been quoted. When media outlets are looking to use you as a source, they will look at those pages to see if you have been used before. When bigger names start to use you as a source, it helps your credibility with other sources and that can open up new opportunities for you as well.

Just remember to take into account the type of publication when you're acting as a source. If it's for a news article, you might say a lot and that can be used to help educate the reporter further about the situation. Ultimately, however, they're only going to take a very small snippet of what you say and put it in the article. Some people have become go-to sources by creating short, catchy comments that go over well. This is particularly important for news and television where there simply isn't a lot of time or space. For other publications, you can be a little more wordy along the way.

In general, I've found that sources appreciate when you give them more info as long as you also provide them with some great one-liners they can throw into the story as well.

Why should you care about being a source? It can only help with publicity for your blog. When the media outlet asks how you want to be quoted, try to use your URL instead of the name of the company. You want it to be very easy for people to find your site if they read your quote. And you'll be amazed at the kind of traffic sites can send you, even small ones.

When I'm able to get my link included in the story, it can sometimes drive more traffic to my site than I can drive myself. This is particularly true with large media outlets, but even more concentrated clicks from a local area can be really beneficial to your traffic stats.

You'll get a big surge of traffic after the article is published or the piece airs on TV. But then, after the fact, you won't return back to where you were originally in terms of traffic. Some of those people who clicked through to your blog will keep coming back for more. Big articles with big links open up your blog to a new audience, and that is exactly the kind of thing that helps you to draw more people in.

If you keep reaching the same people—those already familiar with your blog—an additional link isn't going to drive more traffic sustainably. But if you reach a general news audience or you tap into a group that might not have heard of you before, you're likely to get some of those people to stick with you on a more permanent basis.

The key reason for wanting to be a source is so you can expand your audience. That is not always very easy to do, but when you can do it, your site will benefit tremendously from the exposure.

There are, of course, many other ways to expand your audience. We've talked about several of them above, but there is one big area that we have yet to touch. That's advertising and search engine optimization.

SEO

You're going to get plenty of spam when you start a blog, and one thing that you're going to hear a lot of from these spammers is about search engine optimization or SEO for short. Since spammers like to talk a lot about it, you might assume it's a bunch of hocus-pocus and you shouldn't pay attention. That couldn't be further from the truth. SEO is something very real, but how much time you should spend dealing with it is debatable.

The idea here is to, well, optimize your site for inclusion in search engines. Yes, I know I just twisted the words around to explain what it is, and that's not helpful. I'll explain in greater detail.

After getting direct traffic to your site and referrals from other sites, the greatest way to boost your visits is via search engines. Think about this: How often do you need to find something online? And when you do, how often do you start that search with one of the search engines out there?

The reality is that just about everyone has used Google to search for things. Some people prefer Microsoft's Bing and others prefer Yahoo!. There are other search engines as well, but the point is the same. People go to search engines when they need to find something online unless they know exactly where to go to find it.

Even if people know where to go, they still might use a search engine. I can't tell you how many times I've ended up typing the name of a website into Google instead of just entering the URL myself. People have simply been conditioned to start with search, and that means there is great potential for you to get traffic that way.

People may not know your site, so they aren't going to come directly to you. But let's say you're blogging about electronic gadgets. If someone needs to learn about which tablet to buy, they're going to go to Google and start looking at reviews of different products. You want to be as high up the list of results as possible. Now, for electronic gadgets, that's a very difficult task. There are countless people and sites who are completely devoted to that world, and you're going to have a very difficult time getting to the top of the heap. But there are also a lot more people searching for that topic, and that means some will trickle down as well.

Let's say that, instead, you're blogging about something more off the beaten path. Maybe your area of expertise is air conditioning. Or maybe you are a true expert on replicas from the Roman Empire. These are areas that won't have nearly as much focus as other sites, though they also won't have as much traffic. The goal should be to get your site as high on the list as possible for better visibility and more traffic.

Most will tell you that getting on the first page of search results is the key to success. It is certainly true that the higher up you are in the results, the more visibility you'll have and the more clicks you will receive. But as I stated, you don't need to be on the first page to benefit, especially when there are broad topics with high traffic levels. There are still people who will click beyond the first page, but it's just not as much. Still, every spot you move up the list, the better off you'll be.

With all that in mind, SEO is all about helping your site move up the list to help build traffic. As you can imagine, this can be quite lucrative, so a massive industry has grown around the idea. SEO isn't exactly a science. The search engines change their algorithms from time to time, so there isn't a way to truly know how to work the system. It's a matter of staying on top of changes, if you're truly interested.

You want to know the best way to optimize your site for search engines? That's certainly up for debate. I'll start with my counter-intuitive strategy that I personally employ:

Don't.

That's right. I would suggest that, especially as you get started, you should ignore SEO. This may sound funny. After all, if you're a new site, don't you want to get more people to visit through improved search engine rankings? Yes, but at what cost?

When I talk about cost, I'm not talking about actual monetary cost. Just putting some effort into it yourself can yield some results, but I'm talking about the cost you'll incur in suffering quality.

You're running a blogging business, and the No. 1 thing you can do is produce quality content. If you spend too much time worrying about how to tweak your posts to get the most "juice" with the search engines, that quality is going to suffer. And if the quality suffers, it doesn't matter how many people you bring in to your site, because they aren't going to come back.

Focus on quality.

The best way to get people to come to your site is to have superior content. If you put out something people want to read, then you will attract readers over time. This may not be the strategy if you're looking to get rich quick with some sort of scheme, but if you want a sustainable business, it's the single most important thing you can do.

Easy Ways to Improve SEO

Now that I've sufficiently scared you into focusing on the quality of your content, I'm going to back off my statement a little. There are little things you can do to help with search engine rankings that I would highly recommend. In fact, most blogging software will have some things built in that can help you. Others will also let you install plug-ins to help get some benefit without putting in much effort.

What are all these plug-ins going to do? Well the basic idea of SEO is to make it as easy as possible for search engines to find your content and manipulate the information on your site so that those search engines deem your content to be of as high quality as possible.

A quick web search will help you to identify which plug-ins will help with your blogging software, but here are some of the things that you are going to want to consider. For starters, there are plug-ins that will automatically help to optimize a variety of things on your posts. These can be really helpful because it doesn't impact your content and you don't have to be actively involved.

What actually are we trying to do? A lot of things, actually. In truth, it's a lot of little things that can help.

- When you create a post, there will be a unique link that goes directly to that post, and the information included in that link will help search engines to catalog your content. Some plug-ins can help you optimize the way that you create those links by suggesting words or eliminating unnecessary words like a or the.
- There is also something called "metadata," which isn't viewable directly in the post but does contain information that might help search engines. The value of this data has decreased over the years, but some still argue that it's worth trying to optimize what's in there.
- Links are a big part of SEO. Search engines try to determine the value of your site by looking at the links that come into it. Good quality links help boost the value of the site, and that's why others want you to link to their sites if you have quality content. They want to benefit from a quality link. But links on your own site can end up doing harm if you don't handle them, and that's why there's a way to tell search engines which links to follow and which links not to follow. Plug-ins can help you with that.
- As mentioned, you want to make it easy for search engines to read your site, and one way you can do that is to create a sitemap with all your data in an easy-to-read format (at least, for search engines). This just makes it easier to get your content read. It can also help search engines get your content more quickly. If it doesn't, some plug-ins will help to push the content to the search engines so that they do see it as soon as it's published.
- Images are another area where plug-ins can help. They can remind you to include text describing the image and make it easy to do so. Text around an image is important to help search engines understand the content that's inside.

As you can see, these are mostly technical issues that don't really impact the content people see at all. That's why it can be a good idea to install some of these plug-ins if they don't require much involvement on your part. The problem occurs when you start spending more and more time on SEO and fail to actually focus on the content that really matters. After all, there are only so many hours in a day and you need to prioritize what matters most.

The Hazards of SEO

Where SEO gets really tricky is when you start making changes to your content just to appease the search engine gods. Some people will tell you to focus on using keywords in your posts in order to rank high on search terms that get a lot of traffic. If you aren't careful, this can make your post look like exactly what it is: something written solely to get SEO traffic. This is not going to help you build a sustainable business and will instead make your writing look contrived and stilted. It might help with your SEO practices, but nobody is going to actually want to read it.

That doesn't mean you should ignore keywords. In fact, there are some great tools out there that can help with keywords, but in fact, they can be most useful as idea generators.

When you're blogging, you want to write about what's interesting to you, but it's also nice to think about what's interesting to your readers. Tools like Google Insights and Google Trends can help with that. These sites display information that Google gathers from all its searches. They show you hot search topics, how certain things are trending, and more. For example, if you're a food blogger, you can see what people are searching for and that might inspire you to write a post on those topics.

The top search terms tend to be pretty obvious, because it's headline news. If someone dies of salmonella and it makes the headlines, that will probably shoot to the top of the charts. But once you start digging deeper, you might find surprises. On the day I checked, Girl Scout cookies were the sixteenth-highest search term. That's because it's that time of the year again when the cookies come out for sale, but that might not be top of mind for most bloggers. This can help identify topics people really care about, and then you can write about them. Just don't try to alter your text too much in order to make it fit the mold or you'll shoot yourself in the foot.

Is Your SEO Strategy Working?

A common question in all this is: How do you know if it's even working? Do you have good SEO, whatever that means? There are a few metrics you can use to look at how you rank. The first is the mythical Google PageRank, which you can check at www.prchecker.info. Google's algorithm ranks web pages using a variety of different techniques. The algorithm changes frequently so there's no way to truly crack it, but you can see how your pages rank.

Start with your home page to see where it is on the scale of one to ten. If you get a one, that's not good. If you get a ten, you can retire and go fishing. The number tells you basically how highly your page is valued.

The PageRank you can see is not the exact measurement of how Google values your page, but it's a great way to track your progress. If you move up a notch, that's good for your site. If you move down, it's not. Sometimes, however, a change in your rank isn't due to anything you've done. As stated, Google changes its algorithm from time to time, and that can have either a positive or negative impact. But sometimes, the benefit will be all yours. As you keep writing quality content and people continue linking to your site, you are bound to build a better PageRank as you go.

Another way to see how you're doing is to keep an eye on your analytics software. We talked about this earlier, but there is a specific application here that will help you. Within your analytics software, you can see where your traffic is coming from. It will let you know how many people come in directly, how many come in from other websites, how many people come in from ads, and how many people come in from search engines. If you see a solid increase in the number of visitors coming from search engines, you are probably getting the benefit of better placement. You can play with the software in order to identify trends and see what's really been happening. You might notice that something you did at a certain point in time had a positive or a negative effect. Learn from those occurrences.

If you want more info, there are tools and plug-ins you can use that get into greater detail with your search engine rankings. For WordPress, a tool called SEO Rank Reporter actually tracks Google rankings every three days for the keywords you pick. Want to know how you rank in searches for Girl Scout cookies? This tool will give you the trends.

Once again, I have to caution you not to get too sucked up into the world of SEO. There is going to be a tremendous pull to do a lot of work with SEO to get more traffic, but you can easily get lost in that world. For some, that's why they choose to outsource their SEO work. There are countless numbers of SEO shops that have been set up in the last few years to help you improve your rankings.

Unfortunately, these SEO shops aren't always reputable, and they may promise you things they can't deliver. I mentioned that you'll get a lot of spam from some SEO shops, and this is exactly where that spam comes from. Many of these pop up like the snake oil salesman of yesteryear, and won't provide you with anything except for a way to waste your money.

There are reputable SEO businesses out there, but I would suggest thinking long and hard before deciding if you really need something like this. It may be a nice tool to have down the road, but it's not nearly as important as many of these shops will lead you to believe.

If you do decide to work with a third party to help improve your search engine rankings, the best way to do it is reach out to your network and look for people you know who have had positive experiences with a company. Personal recommendations can go a long way to helping you avoid getting stuck with a terrible experience.

Paying for Advertising

I've written a lot about the creative ways you can grow your site, but there is one way that may sound a little crazy. You can pay for it.

Okay, so that doesn't actually sound crazy at all. It's called advertising, and businesses have done that since the dawn of time. (I believe the creators of fire advertised the invention on cave walls.) There are a lot of different kinds of advertising, but do they all make sense? It's highly unlikely.

Can you imagine buying TV time to advertise your blog during Monday Night Football? I didn't think so. That would probably be insanely overambitious, but hey, if you have money to throw down the tubes, be my guest.

If you plan to start advertising, the first thing you need to do is understand how the advertising systems work. There are several different models out there, and we talked about some when we looked at allowing advertising on your site. The same applies if you flip the circumstances and become the advertiser.

The first thing you should do before you begin paying for advertising is to determine how much you're willing to pay to acquire a reader, or customer. To do that, you need to learn how much a new customer would be worth to you. If you have a blog, he might not be worth much. I mean, clearly you want more readers, but that doesn't mean you can necessarily pay for them.

So, how much is a new reader worth? There are a few ways you could look at this. If you're selling some sort of product or service, it's much easier to determine. What percentage of new readers become paying customers? You'll then have to figure out once they become customers, how much profit do you make off of them? That's how much a customer is worth.

When you're starting your blog, you might want to consider spending more than this single customer is worth, because you think it will help build the site and bring in other customers. That's great. Just make sure you've done the math so you can feel comfortable with the amount of money you're planning to spend.

Once you've decided what a customer is worth, and you've set a budget for an advertising campaign, where should you actually spend it all? Oh sure, there are TV, magazine, and newspaper ads but do you really expect them to bring the kind of traffic you want and need? It might work, but more likely than not, you'll have to spend a very large amount of money and get little in return. Traditional media outlets are incredibly expensive when it comes to advertising.

But there could be some niche opportunities out there. If you write on a topic, maybe you advertise on a popular newsletter, or in a very specific magazine. You could look at trade magazines if you're trying to get to people inside the industry. These are all perfectly legitimate possibilities, if you've reviewed and looked at each one to determine if there will truly be value in them.

That being said, traditional advertising is often simply not going to be worth the amount of money you'll have to put in, at least not for a low-margin business like blogging. Maybe if you sold something that had a higher profit margin, then it would make more sense. But there are most likely going to be other, better ways that you can look to spend your advertising dollars.

Online Advertising

Being an online business means that you should seriously consider targeting your advertising to the online community. After all, with traditional media, you'll reach a large number of people, primarily from older generations, who don't even know what a blog is, let alone read any. If you advertise online, you're going to reach people who spend time online already.

The Internet really allows you to reach a vast audience, but you don't have to. You can specifically target audiences in remarkable ways thanks to the way the Internet has been segmented. There are sites devoted to large swaths of the population (like CNN, ESPN, etc.) and other sites devoted to tiny slivers of the world (which I'll just leave up to your imagination). That means you can specifically target the type of people you want to visit your site in ways that you simply cannot do offline.

Display Advertising

Even though this is all online, you can still look at advertising in traditional ways. There are plenty of opportunities out there for what's called display advertising. That's just when you buy a spot on a site and your advertisement runs there for a certain time.

If you're looking at a small site, you might find details on advertising options or you might not. If not, just e-mail the contact you see on the site. The smaller the site, the less you'll likely have to pay to advertise because there are fewer people there to see it. This isn't 100 percent true. Smaller, highly targeted sites can charge more than bigger sites that are not. The smaller sites know that their readership base is more highly coveted by a small group of advertisers. Either way, you should be able to extract some good value from this type of arrangement.

Paid Search

Display advertising, however, just scratches the surface. While it can do you a lot of good, there is another way to advertise and it's called paid search.

Think about the last time you did a search online. Sure, you got your "native" search results on the page, but you probably also saw a couple that were highlighted at the top of the page, right? I'm guessing there were also a few on the side. Maybe you clicked them or maybe you didn't, but the truth is a lot of people click, and this has become a massive industry.

In fact, Google is the one that really brought the paid-search business model to the mainstream. That's where it makes a killing, and others have tried to replicate that success.

What's so great about paid search? It is incredibly well-targeted because you advertise only on specific search terms. You also don't pay unless someone clicks on your ad, so it can be relatively inexpensive if you want it to be. Anyone can jump into paid search and get it working quickly. It's one of those things that may seem quite daunting at first, but after you try it a few times, it will be very easy to do.

So how exactly does this work? You decide what keywords you like. Let's say you write about chicken farming, so anytime someone searches for "chicken farm," you want them to know you exist. You go to the search engines and work with their paid search options. (Google calls it AdWords, https://adwords.google.com/, and that's the largest network so it's a great place to start.) Once you pick and choose the keywords you want, you have to create an ad to display.

The traditional ad used in paid search has a clickable title, the site URL, and a brief description. This might sound like it would be pretty easy to put together, but you should put a great deal of thought into how you construct the ad. Create something that will convey a sense of trustworthiness but also grabs the eye. It's not nearly as easy as you might hope, but you can explore Google search results to get an idea for how other people do it. Keep in mind that you can't just create one ad and forget about it. You'll want to create different ads depending upon the keywords you buy. Let's say you're an entertainment blogger and you decide to buy ads that will display when people search for "Britney Spears." It would probably be pretty strange if the ad copy said something like "Latest news on Alan Alda" because people searching for Britney Spears aren't going to care. How do you determine where exactly your ad will go on the page? It's a bidding system. You put down how much you're willing to pay, then you get ranked. There is a bit more to it than that, but that's the basic idea. If you pay more, you can get a higher and more prominent placement. If you bid very little, you're likely to be at the bottom of the list, possibly several pages deep. In general, it's better to be higher on the list because you'll get more and higher quality traffic that way.

It makes sense that you get what you pay for. But how exactly do you pay? You just put a certain amount of money into an account up front and funds are deducted as people click on your links. There isn't a flat monthly fee or a cost every time the ad is shown like you might see with the display advertising we talked about earlier. You pay every time someone clicks on that ad, and you pay in real time. (In some cases, you can set it up where you don't pay unless someone completes an action, like purchasing something, but that's not really relevant for bloggers in most cases.)

The way it works is you pay in advance to set up a balance with the ad provider. Then when someone clicks, the amount you've agreed to pay per click is deducted.

This is one great way to budget. Don't put more money into the system than you are willing to spend. Once you run out of money, you can allow it to auto-debit funds, or you can just have it stop. There are plenty of other ways to budget this, including putting a daily limit on it so you don't go overboard.

The way payment is handled with paid search is what makes it so attractive for someone who is just getting started. It allows you to dip your toe in the water while keeping a strict budget and tweaking it along the way. You can spend very little and still see an impact, albeit a small one. But that's okay because at least you're experimenting. You can find out rather quickly if this makes sense for you and you don't have to blow thousands of dollars to figure it out.

You might be tempted to get some outside help on this. It can be overwhelming and time consuming depending upon how much of a campaign you try to mount. At the same time, there are probably thousands and thousands of people out there who would love nothing more than to convince you that you need their help. It's true, there are people who can help you build a paid-search campaign, but you're probably jumping the gun if you're already thinking about working with these people at this point.

Decide What Works For You

I would suggest starting small with Google AdWords (https://adwords.google.com). Even a budget of a few hundred dollars will be enough to get started. (Heck, even fifty dollars is theoretically enough to run a very small test, but I'd do more than that.) Before you start the ads, make sure you've set a budget that's comfortable. Then you can go ahead and open the flood gates. You can shut off a campaign any time and you can alter it as well. Don't be afraid to get creative. Try new keywords, tweak the text in your ads, and pay close attention to the results. You'll quickly learn what works and what doesn't, and you can be the judge of whether or not paid search works for you.

In fact, you should take a step back to make sure any advertising at all works for you. I can tell you that I never paid for advertising for my blog. It was only when I built a related business that I started experimenting with paid search just to see if I could bring in new customers. In general, however, I felt more comfortable working most of the other channels discussed at the beginning of this chapter. Establishing yourself as a credible source and really reaching out to your network can do wonders for your traffic. Paid advertising may not make sense at all, but if you do want to experiment, the easiest way is with paid search because you can control it well on a very limited budget.

Just make sure you take the time to determine exactly what success means if you start with an advertising campaign. Are you happy if you bring in a lot of additional traffic even if it doesn't translate into revenue? Just know what you want to achieve and you'll feel much more comfortable when you start running your tests.

No matter what, when you use any of these techniques, you will be well on your way to expanding the audience that visits your site. You can do a lot to get people to come to your site once, but it's only going to be high-quality content that keeps them coming back.

11

Where Do You Go From Here?

By this point, you should be feeling pretty good about how the business is coming together. You're up and running, all systems are functioning, and you have a growth plan of some sort. As the leader of this business, your work is far from done. It's your responsibility to stay "two steps ahead," as they say. And that means you should keep thinking about what's next.

Should I Stay or Should I Grow?

You've probably figured out that you can build a pretty good business with you at the helm and not much other assistance. It works for some people; those who like the freedom of having their own business and not having to report to others. And those who like not having others feeling dependent upon them. It's the reason a lot of people become writers—it can be a very isolated job for those who prefer it. The freedom is tremendous in that sense.

But for others, it's not enough. Others would rather build out much larger businesses that have many layers to them. It's often a personal preference of the founder of the business, assuming you've created a business that is successful and can be scaled.

This book is about starting a home-based blogging business, and that has all been covered, but it doesn't mean we can't take a peek at what the future might hold, depending upon how you want it to go. The biggest question is around growth and whether or not you want to bother growing. The business ends up being radically different depending upon which way you decide to go. On the one hand, keeping it to yourself gives you ultimate control, but on the other hand, it also means that you have complete responsibility.

Adding Writers

If you start to grow, you'll want to first think about adding writers. Technically, it's a simple procedure. Blogging software allows for multiple users, and you can usually define roles. Some people will be allowed to write and edit their own posts only and don't have the ability to publish. Others can have complete control. You can give increasing levels of responsibility to your new writers as you get more comfortable with them, but you don't have to. You can always have them submit posts to someone with editorial responsibility, if you want to keep strict control.

You can also make it a simple pay-per-post type of commissioning. You don't need to hire full-time staff writers. There are plenty of people out there looking for freelance gigs. You can set the rate you want to pay and find writers with varying levels depending upon what you offer. (For decent quality, you're going to need to pony up, but the rates will depend upon the topic you write about and the demand for writers in that area.)

Before you jump in and get a bunch of new writers, you'll want to ask yourself why you're doing it. Are you having trouble keeping up with the number of posts you need to write and need others to fill in? Or do you think you need to increase the number of posts that go out, so you're just trying to grow beyond where you are today?

These are both legitimate reasons for wanting to bring on new writers. There's no question that when you put out more content, you get more page views. That can mean more advertising dollars. But will it be enough to cover the cost of the additional content?

Can You Afford It and How Will It Affect Your Blog?

It's best to first learn how much money you can make off a page view. Your advertising and product-selling efforts (if any) can be quantified based upon your own posts, and you can make a decision on whether or not you can justify paying the going rate for more content. If you're looking to simply keep up with the level of posting you do today, you might be able to justify paying more for the content than you currently bring in. That's because if you don't keep up a basic level of posting, you're going to lose many of your readers.

In general, however, you shouldn't plan on posting more just for the sake of posting or because you see another site doing it. You need to instead focus on doing what makes sense for you from both a sanity level and a monetary standpoint.

Let's say that you do decide to allow for outside writers. That's going to be a big change for your readership. Even if you don't think you provide a real personality in your writing, you do. And your readers follow your posts because they like what you say and how you say it. When you introduce others into this process, it ends up rocking the boat a little. No matter how hard you try, no two people have identical voices. That can be good. It can help to diversify what's on your site and draw in new readers. But it also has the potential to alienate others.

To offset this, you can make sure you offer easy ways for your readers to follow individual authors. Put out RSS feeds by author so that people can see only the posts from the people they want to follow. Make it clear who writes each post and build personalities around that. It will make it easier for people to stay loyal to those who they like to follow.

Finding The Right Writers

How do you go about deciding who will be a good writer for your site? Without question, you need to request writing samples. Often, those who are professional writers end up making lousy bloggers, because it's completely different. Traditional writers are used to structure and most often write in the third person. Successful blogs (except for blogs about journalism, I'd bet) tend to be more informal and are usually written in the first person. That can be a very difficult transition to make for someone who was trained and has practiced writing in a different way.

That's really up to you, however. You'll know what kind of tone you're trying to achieve, and you would be best served to create a sort of "style guide" for those who write for you. You can talk about everything from expected post lengths to inclusion of imagery and even punctuation use if you so choose. It can be as detailed as you like, realizing that the more detailed it is, the more likely you are to get posts similar to what's already going live on your site.

I will make one distinction here. There is a difference between regular writers and guest posters. Sometimes, a great way to fill in the hole when you can't write is to ask for guest posts. I've used this technique when I've gone on long vacations, when I got married, and when I had my first child. There is rarely a shortage of people interested in writing a guest post for you, especially as you gain a greater following. If you have guest posters, you shouldn't worry as much about making sure there's a perfect fit with your existing content.

Guest Posters

People expect guest posts to be different. Sometimes, you have guest posts from prominent people in your field. Just getting their perspective can be worth it, even if the writing style isn't a perfect fit with what you have on the site. Mark it clearly as a guest post and your readers will be forgiving even if they don't like what they say.

The same doesn't go for frequent writers on staff. That's a very different situation because it has more permanence. People won't want to keep coming back to read if they don't like what a consistent contributor is saying.

That's why I often like to start off relationships with potential writers by using guest posts. It's almost like having an audition, and you can see if your readers receive it well. If it works, you can then make that writer a more permanent fixture. Though I don't have other writers on my blog, I do have some guest posters who have become repeat contributors every couple of months because their posts are so well written and received.

In other words, there are several degrees of having other writers on your site, and you can figure out over time what's best for you. There's no doubt you'll at the very least want guest posts when you have big events in your life, but that might be enough for you. If you do want to expand, however, you will need to consider adding new featured writers. Just be careful when you do.

Building Staff or Keeping Control

It's one thing to add new writers, but if you do you'll need to think about how you can best manage them. Not only do you need to deal with editorial issues, but there are also accounting and employment issues. Who will handle billing and invoicing? Who tracks and issues payments? Who prepares tax documents? It's not nearly as easy as you might think to get someone up and running.

There are plenty of software options out there to help you keep this organized. The behemoth is Quickbooks, which handles accounting and invoicing all in one place. You can do this in a desktop version or you can sign up for Quickbook Online to access your information from anywhere. Other options include Outright for basic accounting and Freshbooks for invoicing. These are just a couple of the many options out there. The more people you add, the more complex your accounting systems will become.

If you add staff you then need to consider a great number of things that might not have applied before. First, you'll need to go through a thorough hiring process.

Once you find a person you like, you'll want to make sure you have a properly pre-pared offer letter. Depending upon your state, you might want to include different things in there. For the most part, you'll want to detail the job description as much as possible. This can be quite intricate, so it's recommended that you work with an attorney who specializes in this area.

An attorney can help you to craft an offer letter that can be used over and over. This person can also help you build out an employee handbook, something you will want to have if you hire someone as an employee. Also, consider what data this person will be handling to determine if additional policies are needed. For example, if you plan on having an employee deal with sensitive customer data like credit cards or social security numbers, you will want a strict policy on how that information is handled.

You need to make sure you protect the data of your customers. In fact, this applies regardless of whether you hire an employee or if you choose to go a different route. When you hire an employee, you enter into a deeper relationship than you do with other types of work contracts. You become responsible for paying the federal payroll tax, and depending upon the hours worked, you might need to provide benefits. For a small business starting out, this can be a very expensive way to get help.

Independent Contractors

Many people look to ways they can use independent contractors to fill in. The idea with an independent contractor is that the person you hire to do work isn't just work-ing for you. That person is self-employed and works for several clients. That person will be responsible for paying all taxes, and you are responsible for issuing IRS form 1099MISC for each independent contractor you hire that makes over six hundred dollars in a year.

Some of these relationships are easy to understand. For example, if you have paid an attorney more than six hundred dollars in a year for services for your business, that is a very clear independent contractor relationship and you must issue a 1099. Some of the other relationships where people do work directly for your business, however, are a bit cloudier.

The IRS gives some guidance on its website at www.irs.gov/businesses/small/article/0,,id=99921,00.html. You don't get to choose whether or not someone is an independent contractor or an employee. It all depends upon what kind of work is being done. In general, if there is a set amount of work at a fixed-pay rate that happens during regular time periods each week, that is an employee. Independent contractors work on a project by project basis. They can decide what work to take and they can do the work at varying times throughout the day. They also must be working for other companies as well.

Understanding Employment Laws

In other words, you can't just go and ask someone to work a nine-to-five job then pay them as an independent contractor, because they aren't. They rely upon you for their employment. This isn't nearly as cut and dry as you might hope, however. There are things like internships, which can look more like employment but are usually for school credit or general experience. These can be paid or unpaid, but they don't fit exactly into either bucket.

If this all sounds confusing, it is. I had one employment lawyer in California tell me that if I decided to hire someone to work for me, I should just prepare to be doing something technically illegal. The rules are so archaic and complex that it's incredibly difficult to be in complete compliance at all times. If that scares you, you're not alone. There are four ways you can try to tackle this issue:

First, you could just get your law degree. I'll go out on a limb and say that's not likely to happen unless you already have it when you start this venture. Otherwise, that's a pretty expensive and time-consuming way to deal with this problem.

Second, you could try to teach yourself the intricacies of employment law in your state through various do-it-yourself books. The information is out there if you want to spend the time. This might require the least cost investment on your part, but the time investment is off the charts. It's also difficult to keep up with changes when you do it this way.

If you do try this path, keep in mind that you won't be under constant scrutiny from the government. Yes, the government is trying to crack down on small businesses illegally classifying employees as independent contractors in order to avoid taxes, but that's not what you're trying to do. (At least, I hope that's not what you're trying to do.) Just do your best to follow the guidelines and if you are told you have done something wrong, you can correct it. There could be penalties depending upon the infraction, but for a very small business that really is trying to do right, you can hope that you won't be penalized too heavily if something is done incorrectly by accident. There is no guarantee, however.

Third, you could hire an employment lawyer to do this work for you. That may sound like a great idea until you realize lawyers charge hundreds of dollars per hour. This makes sense for larger businesses where they have complex employment issues that require greater involvement. A lawyer can be helpful for getting started with things like employee handbooks and offer letters, but it will be hard for you and your small business to justify having a lawyer constantly looking out for what you're doing unless you have a lot of money to spend.

Fourth, you could look at an employment agency of some sort. There are plenty of agencies out there that handle all the details when it comes to hiring. You pay a premium for that employee, but they handle compliance, payroll, etc. It's the way to make your life as easy as possible. But as previously mentioned, you will have to pay extra for this kind of service. If you need staff and don't want to deal with anything around employment rules, however, this is the way to go.

The employment agency actually hires the person and handles all payroll and benefits. Then you pay the employment agency for the services of that person. With a temp agency, you can just pick from their pool of employees, but you probably will want more control than that. That's why you can find the person you want and just work with an agency to handle the employment. It's a simple solution for you, as long as you can justify the costs involved.

Revisiting the Time Commitment

One last thing before we wrap up this book: As you undoubtedly already know, it's going to be a hefty time commitment for you to get this business started. It's that way with every single small business at the beginning. It also usually continues that way permanently unless you bring in new employees, or limit the scope of your business. That's the life of a small business owner.

I would suggest revisiting the time commitment every few months to make sure you're still motivated and providing the highest-quality content you can. It's easy to burn out in this business, and that's the last thing you want to do.

Check in with your family and yourself on set occasions and revisit whether or not this business is working as planned and whether or not you're able to make it run without killing yourself. If not then you either need to think about adding new people to take the burden off, find a way to reduce the output, or simply try something different.

Writing a blog can be incredibly rewarding. You will develop a great following, you can find yourself influencing the topic at hand over time, and you can build a community you really get to know. The discussion it generates is fantastic, and you truly can have an impact. That's not something everyone can say.

The lifestyle of a home-based business is one that many people love, while others have trouble adjusting to the blending of their home and business lives. Make sure that this is the right type of business for you before you devote your full resources to the project.

Keep in mind that as a blogger, you're always going to be looking for more stories, more topics to cover. It becomes a full-time job one way or another since your brain will always be searching for ways to improve your output. It's truly a fantastic thing.

I personally wish you much success in getting your blog up and running. Thanks for your time, and I hope that this book has been helpful in getting you on your way.

Appendix: Resources

Accounting Software Providers

Outright: www.outright.com

Quicken: www.quicken.com

QuickBooks: www.quickbooks.com

WaveAccounting: www.waveaccounting.com

WorkingPoint: www.workingpoint.com

Affiliate Program Managers

AffiliateManager: www.affiliatemanager.com

Commission Junction: www.cj.com

FlexOffers.com: www.flexoffers.com

LinkShare: www.linkshare.com

Business Registration Search

Alabama: http://www.sos.alabama.gov/vb/inquiry/inquiry.
aspx?area=Business%20Entity

Alaska: http://commerce.alaska.gov/CBP/Main/

Arizona: http://starpas.azcc.gov/scripts/cgiip.exe/WService=wsbroker1/
connect.p?app=names-report.p

Arkansas: http://www.sos.arkansas.gov/corps/search_all.php

California: http://kepler.sos.ca.gov/

Colorado: http://www.sos.state.co.us/biz/BusinessEntityCriteriaExt.do

Connecticut: http://www.concord-sots.ct.gov/CONCORD/index.jsp

Delaware: https://delecorp.delaware.gov/tin/GINameSearch.jsp

Florida: https://www.myfloridalicense.com/wl11.asp

Georgia: http://corp.sos.state.ga.us/corp/soskb/csearch.asp

Hawaii: http://hbe.ehawaii.gov/documents/search.html

Idaho: http://www.sos.idaho.gov/corp/corindex.htm

Illinois: http://www.ilsos.gov/corporatellc/

Indiana: http://www.in.gov/sos/business/2436.htm

Iowa: http://sos.iowa.gov/search/business/(S(oodsud55cqdad2umdqikpdrq))/search.aspx

Kansas: http://www.kansas.gov/bess/

Kentucky: https://app.sos.ky.gov/ftsearch/

Louisiana: http://www.sos.la.gov/tabid/819/Default.aspx

Maine: https://icrs.informe.org/nei-sos-icrs/ICRS?MainPage=x

Maryland: http://sdatcert3.resiusa.org/UCC-Charter/CharterSearch_f.aspx

Massachusetts: http://www.sec.state.ma.us/cor/functionality/search.htm

Michigan: http://www.michigan.gov/statelicensesearch

Minnesota: http://mblsportal.sos.state.mn.us/

Mississippi: https://business.sos.state.ms.us/corp/soskb/csearch.asp

Missouri: http://www.sos.mo.gov/BusinessEntity/

Montana: https://app.mt.gov/bes/

Nebraska: http://www.nebraska.gov/sos/corp/corpsearch.cgi

Nevada: http://nvsos.gov/sosentitysearch/

New Hampshire: http://www.sos.nh.gov/corporate/soskb/csearch.asp

New Jersey: http://www.njportal.com/DOR/businessrecords/

New Mexico: http://web.prc.newmexico.gov/Corplookup/
(S(dg5pqgf1foi4qvegemajnhm5))/CorpSearch.aspx

New York: http://www.dos.ny.gov/corps/bus_entity_search.html

North Carolina: http://www.secretary.state.nc.us/corporations/csearch.aspx

North Dakota: http://www.nd.gov/sos/businessserv/registrations/
business-search.html

Ohio: http://www2.sos.state.oh.us/pls/bsqry/f?p=100:1

Oklahoma: http://www.sos.ok.gov/business/corp/records.aspx

Oregon: http://egov.sos.state.or.us/br/pkg_web_name_srch_inq.login

Pennsylvania: http://www.corporations.state.pa.us/corp/soskb/csearch.asp

Rhode Island: http://ucc.state.ri.us/CorpSearch/CorpSearchInput.asp

South Carolina: http://www.scsos.com/search%20business%20ofilings

South Dakota: http://sdsos.gov/Business/Search.aspx

Tennessee: http://tnbear.tn.gov/ECommerce/FilingSearch.aspx

Texas: http://ourcpa.cpa.state.tx.us/coa/Index.html

Utah: https://secure.utah.gov/bes/action

Vermont: http://www.sec.state.vt.us/seek/keysrch.htm

Virginia: http://www.scc.virginia.gov/clk/bussrch.aspx

Washington: http://www.sos.wa.gov/corps/corps_search.aspx

West Virginia: http://apps.sos.wv.gov/business/corporations/

Wisconsin: http://www.wdfi.org/apps/CorpSearch/Search.aspx?

Wyoming: https://wyobiz.wy.gov/Business/FilingSearch.aspx

Forming a Corporation

LegalZoom: www.legalzoom.com/incorporation-guide/forming-a-corporation.html

Nolo: www.nolo.com/legal-encyclopedia/form-corporation-how-to-
incorporate-30030.html

ProBlogger: www.problogger.net/archives/2008/07/07/should-you-incorporate/

Small Business Administration: www.sba.gov/category/navigation-structure/ starting-managing-business/starting-business/establishing-business/ inc

Free Analytics Providers

AWStats: www.awstats.org

Google Analytics: www.google.com/analytics

Site Meter: www.sitemeter.com

Webalizer: www.mrunix.net/webalizer/

Hosts

DreamHost: www.dreamhost.com

FatCow: www.fatcow.com

InMotion: www.inmotionhosting.com

Pair Networks: www.pair.com

Yahoo! Web Hosting: www.smallbusiness.yahoo.com/webhosting

Industry Research Tools

Alexa: www.alexa.com

Alltop: www.alltop.com

Blog Catalog: www.blogcatalog.com

Google: www.google.com

Technorati: www.technorati.com

Wayback Machine: www.web.archive.org

Merchandise Sites

CafePress: www.cafepress.com

PrintMojo: www.printmojo.com

Spreadshirt: www.spreadshirt.com (limited to clothing)

Zazzle: www.zazzle.com

Photo Hosts

Facebook: www.facebook.com

Flickr: www.flickr.com

ImageShack: www.imageshack.us

Picasa: www.picasa.google.com

SmugMug: www.smugmug.com

Stock Photo Sites

Dreamstime: www.dreamstime.com

Getty Images: www.gettyimages.com

iStockphoto: www.istockphoto.com

Jupiter Images: www.jupiterimages.com

Shutterstock: www.shutterstock.com

Glossary

We've talked about a lot of different terms and acronyms in this book that might seem foreign to you. For that reason, I've put together a handy glossary for quick reference. Here are some terms that you might need to look up.

articles of organization: Often required as part of the formation of your business entity. Banks may request this when you try to set up a new business account.

accrual accounting: When you record sales when money is earned, as opposed to cash accounting when you record sales when money is actually received.

analytics: The process of measuring the performance of your site in terms of number of visitors, where they come from, and other details. This is important for advertising and for measuring your success.

blogroll: A list usually displayed in a sidebar on your site with links to blogs you like.

cash accounting: When you record sales when money is received, as opposed to accrual accounting when you record sales when money is earned.

code of ethics: A page on your website that describes your policy of ethics; includes accepting payment, gifts, and full disclosure of potential conflicts.

commenters: Readers of your blog who decide to participate in the conversation on your site through a mechanism you provide.

cost per acquisition (CPA): Advertising method that pays you when the person you refer completes a purchase from the advertiser.

cost per click (CPC): Advertising method that pays you when someone on your site clicks on the advertising link to go the advertiser site.

cost per thousand impressions (CPM): Advertising method that pays based on the number of times you display the ad on your blog.

Creative Commons: A licensing method that allows you to use third-party content on your site with limited restrictions. This usually requires a link back to the original work and may require that you also license it the same way.

directory: A page on your website that acts as a resource for readers looking for companies to do business with in areas related to your content. This can be a paid directory where advertisers must pay you for inclusion.

display advertising: Ads that are usually shown next to your content with images, text, etc. On blogs, this is usually thought of as CPM advertising.

Doing Business As (DBA): If you operate your business under a different name than the officially registered name, you can file a DBA with your local government that shows the names under which you operate (also known as a Fictitious Business Name).

fair use: Refers to the limited use of copyrighted material on your own site in order to comment on it or use for discussion purposes.

Federal Tax Identification Number: Businesses must apply to the US Internal Revenue Service (online is okay) for a number for tax purposes.

Fictitious Business Name: If you operate your business under a different name than the officially registered name, you can file a fictitious business name with your local government that shows the names under which you operate (also known as Doing Business As).

freelance-style agreement (pay per post): When you pay someone a fixed amount to write something for your site.

freemium model: When you provide a certain level of content for free but you offer greater access for a fee.

impression: Each time a page on your site is displayed on someone's device (also known as page view).

Limited Liability Company (LLC): A form of business entity that protects you personally from liability, can be solely owned or owned by multiple "members" of the entity.

margin model: When you focus on making more money per person off a small reader base, as opposed to the volume model.

microblogging: Most commonly known as Twitter; small bursts of information instead of longer-form traditional blog posts.

ombudsmen: People who try to help resolve issues on behalf of readers thanks to their better connections within the industry and their ability to air issues publicly.

page view: Each time a page on your site is displayed on someone's device (also known as an impression).

paid search: When you pay for text-ad placement alongside online search results; commonly known as search engine marketing, or SEM.

plug-in: Many blogging platforms allow users to customize their installations by using plug-ins to bring additional functionality.

podcasting: An audio form of blogging where people record conversations and post them publicly.

public domain: When a work is no longer copyrighted and can be used freely by anyone.

rights managed: A photo license method that allows you to use the purchased image for one specific use; may or may not be exclusive.

royalty free: A photo license method that allows you to use the purchased image for multiple uses per the guidelines of the license; always nonexclusive.

RSS (Really Simple Syndication): Puts your content into a stripped-down, machine-readable file that makes it easy to for readers to see your content in different formats on different viewers.

search engine marketing (SEM): You pay for text ad placement alongside online search results, also known as paid search.

search engine optimization (SEO): An effort to have your site shown toward the beginning of search results when people search for relevant topics, SEM is sometimes lumped into this.

search engine ranking: The point, or rank, at which your site is displayed in search results online. It is best to be No. 1, the first result people will see.

self-hosted blog: When you pay to have your site live virtually at a web host, in contrast with third party-hosted blog.

terms of use: The rules you post on your site that apply to anyone who comes to read your content or use your site in any way.

third party-hosted blog: When your blogging software also hosts the blog for you on its own servers, in contrast with self-hosted blog.

volume model: When you focus on making less money per person off a large reader base, as opposed to the margin model.

Index

About the Author

Brett Snyder is the author of the award-winning consumer air-travel blog The Cranky Flier (crankyflier.com). Brett has worked for multiple airlines including America West and United in a variety of functions including revenue management, marketing, and strategy. On his blog, he focuses on explaining to travelers why the airlines do what they do from the perspective of someone who has been on the inside and understands it well.  The result is Brett now works full-time as President and Chief Airline Dork of Cranky Flier LLC.

Brett's success with The Cranky Flier has led to other opportunities to complement his work, including an air travel column for CNN.com alongside writing for *Condé Nast Traveler* and Intuit's Small Business Blog. In 2009, he started his Cranky Concierge (crankyconcierge.com) air-travel assistance business as a complement to the blog and it has grown quickly.

Brett has appeared on radio and television programs on CNN, Bloomberg Television, and NPR-affiliated stations among others. He is regularly quoted as an airline expert in news media including the *New York Times*, the *Wall Street Journal*, and in many local papers. He is also known internationally. In the UK, The Cranky Flier was named one of the fifty most powerful blogs in the world by *The Observer Magazine*.

The credibility he has built using The Cranky Flier as a platform has allowed him to make a good living doing what he loves. Visit him at crankyflier.com and crankyconcierge.com.